SUE H

MW01516637

snobs,
nobs
and # yobs

a classy guide to Australia

Lothian
B O O K S

Acknowledgement

The author and publisher acknowledge the use of the lines, 'Does your Dad own a brewery?' and 'Do you fuck on first dates?' from Kevin Bloody Wilson's song 'Kev's Courtin' Song', from the album, *Kev's Back*, copyright © Kevin Bloody Wilson, 1985.

Thomas C. Lothian Pty Ltd
11 Munro Street, Port Melbourne, Victoria 3207

Copyright © Sue Hart-Byers 1999
First published 1999

All rights reserved. No part of this publication may be reproduced, stored in a retrieval system or transmitted in any form by any means without the prior permission of the copyright owner. Enquiries should be made to the publisher.

National Library of Australia
Cataloguing-in-Publication data

Hart-Byers, Susan.
Snobs, nobs and yobs: a classy guide to Australia.
ISBN 0 7344 0043 8.
1. Social classes – Australia – Humour.
2. Australian wit and humour.
305.50994

Design by Paulene Meyer
Cartoons by John Ward, Pictureplane
Cover design by P.A.G.E. Pty Ltd
Printed in Australia by Griffin Press Pty Limited

Contents

Preface

A rich woman and a poor woman happened to end up next to each other in the labour ward. The rich woman couldn't stop talking.

'My husband is so pleased with me when I have a baby that he always buys me a wonderful present,' she said to the poor woman.

'That-th nith,' said the poor woman.

'Yes,' said the rich woman, 'After our first baby was born he bought me this beautiful diamond ring.'

'That-th nith,' said the poor woman.

'And after our second baby he bought me a new car.'

'That-th nith,' said the poor woman.

'And after this baby he is going to take me on an expensive cruise,' said the rich woman.

'That-th nith,' said the poor woman.

'Tell me,' said the rich woman, 'Does your husband buy you anything after you have children?'

'Yeth,' said the woman, 'After my latht baby wath born he paid for me to have elocuthion lethonth.'

'Oh,' said the rich woman, 'That's very nice, isn't it? But they, ah, don't seem to have worked very well, do they?'

'Yeth they have,' said the poor woman. 'I uthed to thay "Fuck Off!" Now I thay, "That-th nith."'

Anyone who finds this joke offensive would be well advised not to read this book, because you will find it annoyingly politically incorrect (that is, truthful) from beginning to end. Everyone is entitled to their own opinion, so I simply say to you, 'That-th nith.'

Introduction:
Class system.
What class system?

Caroline from the leafy suburbs thinks that Nikki's very new house is vulgar. Nikki thinks that Caroline is a pretentious bore. Dot from the outer suburbs is disgusted by Sharon next door's dirty messy house. Sharon laughs at Dot's husband Brian, calling him an old woman. Barb in-the-middle looks down slightly on Dot, but finds much to admire in Caroline. Sascha, enjoying her trendy inner-city life, feels superior to her suburban family and childhood friends. Virginia and Wolfgang can't help despising anyone who doesn't have a degree. John and Sally from the country think that all city people are softies and therefore of a lower caste.

Clearly, what is needed is an explanation of our class system. Undoubtedly, there are those who are already aware of the finer points and can immediately recognise the significance of a pair of rubber thongs or a wicker picnic basket and are able to place the owners in their exact spot in the social hierarchy, but others need more help.

This book goes even further. It not only describes the different groups, but advises which are the desirable classes and which aren't. And finally, it suggests *what you can do* to become a member of the class of your choice.

There's absolutely no need to feel guilty about this. Ask yourself — if people don't want to be identified as belonging to a particular class, why do they do everything they can to be seen as such? Why do Lower Middle lounge rooms look the same all over the country? Why does Mrs Middle Australia buy *exactly* the same clothes whether she lives in Geelong or Wagga, Toowoomba or Burnie? Have you noticed how a Real Aussie mother shouting at her kids in the Sydney supermarket sounds uncannily like the one doing the same in Elizabeth?

In any case, class consciousness, whatever the serious social analysts may say, has little to do with putting others down and is more a case of 'counting your blessings'. When people notice that someone is a little lower down the social scale than themselves, this is not usually because they have any grudge against other classes, but simply that it makes *them* feel better.

And, the wish to move even further up the social ladder is a purely self-centred, egotistical and totally understandable wish to take advantage of our fluid class system. People do it every day.

ONE

Stuck up

*Snob: a person seeking to imitate or associate
with those of superior rank or wealth*

The word 'snob' is misunderstood by many. It is often used completely incorrectly, especially by insecure people from the Lower Middle class. They think it means 'up yourself', whereas it really means 'terrified of being left out'. Everyone is a snob about something, even the people who argue most loudly against the class system. It's amazing how quickly people lose their prejudices once they themselves have achieved some success.

THINGS YOU SHOULD KNOW

- The most important element of our class structure is style. Background counts for less and less every day. Even money, while always desirable, is not so important as is often supposed. What matters is how you earn and spend your money rather than how much you have. Where you live, what you eat or wear, what car you drive, who you vote for, what sport you follow, who your friends are, where your children go to school, your tastes and interests are what count.

- It doesn't much matter which part of Australia you live in, although it is true that there are some regional differences. As a general rule of thumb, the hotter the climate the lower the class.

- Race and ethnic background are less important than people imagine. While some of the stereotypes contain a grain of truth — you won't find too many Jewish South Africans living quiet impoverished suburban lives — there are people from all countries in every class.

- No class is completely set, not even the Upper Class. However, some are more reluctant than others to let newcomers in.

- As you move up the social ladder (few people plan to go down), don't lie too much about your background because you are bound to be found out, especially if you become famous. If there's little chance of your family appearing on the scene very often, then say nothing. If they are highly visible you are better to praise them to the skies. 'Mum is marvellous. We all adore her.' Never apologise for your parents' lack of taste, class, etc.

- Understand that despite the fact that there is nothing wrong with being a snob, it is crucial not to appear to be one. You won't be accepted if anyone thinks you're trying too hard. The trick is to appear to be a natural born member of the class you are aspiring to join. You belong.

TWO

What's what

There are many classes in Australia — it's not just a matter of moving up from lower to upper. If you're moving up, what are you moving up to? Each class has its own conventions and subculture. We're not talking about tiny variations in fashion — what's in or out this year, as decided by the glossy magazines — but the broader picture. To fit in, you may have to reinvent yourself from start to finish.

Wherever you live in Australia, these are the groups you will encounter most: **Real Aussie, Lower Middle, Upper Middle, Seriously Rich, Intellectual, Inner-City Sophisticate, Country** and **Middle Australia**. Some of these are more desirable than others. In particular, aspiring snobs don't want to be mistaken for Lower Middle or Real Aussie.

REAL AUSSIES

This is the closest to being a classless class. Often confused with poor subclass. This is false, despite surface similarities in dress, speech and habits. Real Aussies have jobs and money. Can be Real Aussie whether you're a worker in a factory or the owner of the factory. Obvious traps here for the social climber — making a bit of money and buying the latest big screen TV *does not* make you upper class.

Relationship to other classes

Real Aussie is in another category altogether to the other classes in that it runs almost parallel to all of them. More money than the Lower Middles, and not as prissy. Similar assets to Middle Australians, but louder and more chaotic lifestyle. Possible to go on to become Seriously Rich. However, nothing in common with Intellectuals, Upper Middles or Inner-City Sophisti-cates (except may work for them). Often found in the country.

LOWER MIDDLE

This class is the great watershed point of the Australian class system. Most misunderstood class of all. Despite its large size, often overlooked by those commenting on social trends — as though everybody in the country lives a glamorous life in an inner-city apartment, going to trendy cafés for breakfast. (Many people do, of course, and you may hope to be among them, but you won't find any Respectable Suburbanites there.)

It is vital that any aspiring snob be able to recog-nise this class at a glance because it can be most deceptive. Many people escaping from a Real Aussie or poor background think they've made it when they acquire a safe job in the bank and start paying off a neat suburban house. They haven't. It's also useful to know whether you are in any danger of marrying someone from this class.

Relationship to other classes

Antagonistic relationship with Real Aussies. (They live in the same suburbs.) Related to many Middle Australians. Young Respectable Suburbanites often become Middle Australian or Inner-City Sophisticates. May be Country. Little in common with Upper Middles or Intellectuals.

UPPER MIDDLE

This one is a popular choice, the class to which many people aspire, although it is often confused with Seriously Rich or even Upper Class. Upper Middles very aware of their own place in the hierarchy, but not averse to out-siders thinking they have higher status. With the Upper Class they play up their own importance so they don't feel like poor relations. With other classes they play it down, partly so as not to appear to be showing off, partly to show that they know more about the class system than anybody else (that is, they are more successful snobs).

Relationship to other classes

Upper Middles may have started as Middle Australians, Intellectuals or Inner-City Sophisticates. Possible to move up from poor (a long haul). Mix with Seriously Rich at school events, some charity and private func-tions. More in common with Intellectuals. May well be Country. Amused by Lower Middles. Know Real Aussies as cleaners, gardeners, tradesmen.

SERIOUSLY RICH

The Seriously Rich can also be confused with Upper Class or Upper Middles. Unfortunately, flamboyant and irresponsible lifestyle can give everyone a bad name. Comes from sudden accumulation of cash leading to light-headedness and arrogance leading to a feeling of invincibility and immunity from censure. Sometimes compounded by society in general, which has no expectations that the rich will contribute in any meaningful way.

Relationship to other classes

Over time, dismissal as lightweights begins to annoy so the rich sober up and start worrying about the state of the nation. They change their habits, tastes, attitudes and so on and after a generation or so no longer *are* Seriously Rich (which isn't to say they don't have money) but either Aussie aristocracy or Upper Middle. The Seriously Rich class is therefore as fluid as Middle Australia. It's a halfway house, a limbo, on the way up from poor, Lower Middle or Real Aussie. In the meantime, members despise all other classes except Upper Middle. Many Real Aussie men aspire to be Seriously Rich.

INTELLECTUAL

Intellectual is a most useful class. For anyone who wants to escape Lower Middle, poor, or Middle Australia but doesn't have the money or inclination to make it into

Upper Middle, this can be a safe option. Not even considered snobs because of their avowed disgust with the class system. In truth, while they talk a great deal about tolerance they are one of the least tolerant groups of all. Anybody who doesn't think like them is, frankly, an idiot.

Relationship to other classes

The other classes wouldn't be worried by this intolerance, except that Intellectuals have such a lot to say about everything. Close relationship with Upper Middles. Many young Intellectuals grow up to become Upper Middles. Great admiration for poor. Loathe Upper Class and Seriously Rich. Despise Inner-City Sophisticates but some tastes in common with them. Nothing in common with Country. Admire Real Aussies in theory but not in practice.

INNER-CITY SOPHISTICATE

Another common name for this group is 'Yuppie', a word which has caused great confusion and needs to be clarified here. Dreamed up in the eighties to explain the apparent rise of a new class, it is supposed to be an acronym for Young Upwardly Mobile Professional. However, these initials make the word YUMP, which is unfortunate. The word Yuppie is often ignorantly applied to Upper Middles who aren't so much on the way up as firmly settled in the class of their choice.

Relationship to other classes

These are mostly younger people trying to escape poor, Lower Middle or Real Aussie. Mix with Intellectuals in cafés, theatres and at openings, but exasperated by their dress sense. Also some contact with Upper Middles and Seriously Rich at big occasions. No point of contact with Country — they speak a foreign language. Consider themselves above Middle Australians — middles don't care.

COUNTRY

This class has been the most enduringly popular of Australian lifestyles, although the form has changed over the years. Used to be the wish of many to be rich farmer — low wool prices ended that. The back-to-nature, self-sufficiency fantasy has also died a natural death. It harks back to the sixties, to hippies and communes. Those who tried it found that making their own mud bricks and milking the goat every day was less amusing than it sounded. The current version is more of the hobby farm, weekend farmer, let's-do-it-in-comfort style.

Relationship to other classes

Like Real Aussies, Country class runs parallel to the others. Country people can be almost any class except Inner-City Sophisticates or Intellectual. However, while many Lower Middle, Middle Australian and Real Aussie people live in the country already, those aspiring to it tend to think Upper Middle. They share a similar taste in clothes and outlook on life.

MIDDLE AUSTRALIA

This is the largest of all the classes, for obvious reasons. We are, on the whole, a democratic wealthy country, so the Middle Class is bound to be larger than in countries with a few immensely rich rulers and a vast mass of starving peasants. As well, our prosperity leads to many people being able to call themselves Middle Class who in other countries might be Lower Middle or even Working Class.

But why do so many people *wish to be considered* Middle Class? Answer: Because the Middle Class is the class of compromise. Most men are Real Aussies by natural inclination. Women yearn towards Upper Middle. Rather than fighting it out, Middle Australian couples sensibly compromise on neutral ground.

Relationship to other classes

Middle Australia is the middle child, the link. May have connections with every other class.

TOP AND BOTTOM

There are two classes that have been left out. They are the very poor (the welfare recipients) and the very rich and powerful.

The nobs

The nearest thing we have to an aristocracy, the so-called 'squattocracy' (which also includes the successful manufacturing and retailing families, or at least the ones who have had their money for several generations), is not described in detail.

The main reason is that this is the one class which it is very hard to break into. It's often assumed that women can marry into it, but it is extremely difficult. However beautiful and well-spoken you may be, if you aren't one of them, he's unlikely to marry you. He may well adore you and live with you for years but when it comes to basics, when it's time he settled down to produce an heir, you'll be gone, with — if you can wangle it — a generous settlement to remember him by. He, meanwhile, will marry some well-connected girl whom he's known since childhood. (When you're older and rich and important in your own right, you may get away with it.)

It's even harder for men. However much money you make you'll still be Seriously Rich, not old money. Your grandchildren may crack society, but you won't. It's also almost impossible for men to marry into the aristocracy. In the unlikely event of you getting some gorgeous squattocrat girl to the altar she will become whatever class you are. You won't join hers. It won't be very long before she despises you for this and will leave you for one of her own while everyone immediately and conveniently forgets your name.

It's not impossible to enter the ranks of the elite — they have to replenish the stock occasionally — but only a very few will be amongst the chosen.

The battlers

The poor, or 'subclass' as they are often called, are also omitted. They are written about *ad nauseam* already and are probably heartily tired of hearing about themselves. One view has it that they are the scum of the earth on whom all of society's problems can be blamed. The other is that they are poor unfortunate victims whose misfortunes are a consequence of the ills of society. Whatever, the fact is no one in their right mind would choose to be one of them so they don't appear here. They used to be called the Working Class, but as most of them now aren't working, when they are mentioned in passing they are simply called 'the poor'.

These two are the classes which appear most often in the newspapers, sometimes for remarkably similar reasons — sex and crime (not for nothing do journalists know only two words to describe houses: 'modest' or 'luxury'), but they aren't featured in this book except in passing.

THREE

Kev and Sharon: Real Aussies

*Alternative names: ockers, yobbos, rough
diamonds, salt of the earth, plebs*

If you're not of this class yourself, you won't have any trouble spotting it — it is much more visible, for instance, than the Lower Middle Class. The Real Aussie is louder, brighter, showier. They seem to be everywhere — dragging their Eskys into every sporting event under the sun, kicking sand all over you at the beach, crunching and munching away at the cinema. Above all, Real Aussies are highly noticeable at the supermarket, with their booming voices and their squawking, squabbling children.

However, if you are an Aussie yourself it can be difficult to see yourself as such, or to think that there is anything wrong with it if you do. After all, you're not a layabout dole bludger, you don't beat up complete strangers (although you're certainly prepared to defend yourself when necessary), you've never been in jail. You own your own house and your children have every toy under the sun.

Kev and Sharon in a rare moment of meaningful communication

ARE YOU A YOB?

The look

The key word is casual. Some other classes — in particular
the up-themselves Upper Middles — think you're boring
and conservative (remembering white socks with dark
trousers and brylcreemed hair — a look you left behind
years ago), but that is to forget your 'Who cares? Stuff
everybody, I'll do what I like,' attitude to what you wear
to the supermarket. Would any of the other classes be
seen anywhere in tight floral leggings, a short T-shirt and
bare feet?

Kev

Kev is the ocker portrayed in cartoons. If you are prepared to wear a blue singlet, Stubby shorts (showing your backside), and thongs in public you are probably a Real Aussie. If you have even one tattoo and a bandy-legged walk then there's no question about it. For a barbecue or the pub on a Saturday night you would add a T-shirt. In winter Ugg boots and jeans.

To get dressed up for something like a wedding, Kev wears trousers that are slightly out of date in cut, a white shirt and a borrowed tie. An older man will have one suit, a younger one might have some sort of jacket, but not necessarily.

Kev's son Donny (from his brief first marriage) and his mates always wear the fashion of their particular subculture. Outsiders may believe that all teenagers look similarly scruffy, but members of groups like the rappers, technos, surfies, Gothics, ferals, grunges, alternatives or teenyboppers recognise minute differences of dress or behaviour (even if Sharon thinks they know nothing about nothing).

Sharon

There are two basic looks for older women: fat, defeated, it's all too much effort, or thin, weathered and wiry. In neither case does the older Real Aussie woman wear make-up or jewellery. She also wears thongs or sandals most of the time, rather than shoes, partly because of her bunions. She hardly ever wears pantyhose. If she lives in the tropics she never wears them. She doesn't own a tailored jacket of any description, but has several sweatshirts and a plastic raincoat.

A look much favoured among older women is that of a perm and a dye half-grown out of the hair. Some go for just the perm growing out — dead straight halfway down the head and then frizz. It's puzzling that anyone would find this attractive; it can't be a matter of cost, because cutting it all off would be far cheaper in the long run than perming and dyeing.

Younger Aussie girls are much more glamorous than their mothers or husbands. Sharon's unmarried friend Kylie wears short skirts and high strappy sandals, little tight tops and jeans in the latest style. Everything is synthetic and in very bright colours. She wears a lot of make-up and jewellery (not real). Hairstyles are elaborate and based on lots of hair ornaments. For some reason a typical style is hair drawn up on top in a scrunchy, with a ponytail at the back. As well, there might be a couple of clips or bows of various kinds. Hair can be any colour but will always be a definite colour. Blonde is yellow, dark is jet-black, red is scarlet.

Sharon looks smarter than her mother and aunts, but not as sexy as before she was married — Kev doesn't like to think his mates might see her tits. None of them would dare to say she looked good because Kev would thump them. Most of the time she wears jeans but her favourite outfit for special outings is a leather skirt, lacy top, high-heeled sandals and lots of hair.

The house

Outside

Just walking to Kev and Shar's front door is something of a health risk, as there are so many things to fall over. The front yard looks as though a cyclone has gone through, picking everything up and dropping it down again in random order. A car is lying on the lawn in an advanced state of disrepair, the length of the grass growing up around it showing how long it's been there.

There are three bikes, two of them in working order, albeit rusty, and a wheelbarrow with no wheel. A motorbike in very good condition takes up the middle of the garage while the car, a big V8, is out on the concrete driveway. It is difficult to see the driveway because it is covered in oil. There is a pile of sand in one corner of the yard with grass beginning to grow over it. Timber, bits of metal, car parts and various chewed up plastic bottles (the dogs) are scattered here and there.

The house itself could be of many different styles but is most likely to be of seventies design — dark brick, with an odd-shaped roof and one big window of yellow glass. There is no garden as such but along the fence line are a few flowers, possibly carnations, held up with stakes, and one or two trees which look as though they need fertilising.

As you approach the front door the dogs start barking and continue for the next couple of hours.

Inside

As you walk in the door the first thing that hits you is the smell. This turns out to be mostly dog-smell, but also comes from the pizza scraps lying around on the lounge room floor. As well, Shar leaves ashtrays all over the house. Kev says she bloody smells like one. Sharon says that she would give up but she's not going to be told what to do by bloody do-gooders, thank you very much.

The hall floor is hard shiny tiles. There is a small telephone table covered with a pile of unironed clothes. The phone is on the floor. You step down into the lounge room which has a pale green carpet in a tufted synthetic fabric. One whole corner of the room is taken up with an enormous brown velvet modular couch on which Kev's mate Big Red is lying, sound asleep at midday. In another corner a very large TV is showing a footy match, loudly. On the floor are six pizza packets, empty beer cans, Coke bottles, car magazines and many kids' toys, some of them in one piece.

There is a sideboard next to the TV containing bottles of brightly coloured fluid — liqueurs of one sort or another. There is also an assortment of glasses and china, all liberally decorated with gold rims. Some of them have gold lettering as well. On top of the sideboard are examples of the cruder souvenirs that can be bought in Fiji and Surfers Paradise (where Kev and Shar went for their honeymoon). Penises and naked women feature strongly.

The dining room contains a pool table on which are piled even more clean but unironed clothes. In one corner of this room is the bar which has pub mirror tiles behind it, an enormous collection of glasses and drinks of every kind. Kev almost always drinks beer, but his Dad likes a shot of rum now and then. Several plaques containing witty sayings are hung on one wall.

The kitchen is modern and well-equipped but spectacularly messy. The dishwasher stopped working three weeks ago and dishes have been piling up ever since. As well as plates and cutlery and pots and pans on every surface there are empty food cans, an overflowing rubbish bag, and a few greasy car parts. Kev is just waiting for Sharon to say something about them so he has an excuse to have a good row. The meals area has a table covered in half-eaten meals, an enormous plastic container of salt and a bottle of tomato sauce.

In the family room another TV is blaring. Three children are sitting in front of it, but are too busy shoving and swearing at each other to actually watch the programme. The only furniture in this room is several bean-bags, most of which are spilling their beads all over the floor. Jaylene thumps Aaron and the noise reaches dangerous levels.

The main bedroom has a large bed, unmade, and built-in robes of mock rosewood with clothes falling out all over the floor. One of the minor bedrooms is currently being used as a store room and is packed to the roof with things that Sharon has been meaning to throw out for years.

The back garden

This is mostly covered in brown paving bricks with various complicated fences and gates for the dogs. There is a kidney-shaped fibreglass pool. It's one of Sharon's many jobs to keep it clean and in running order.

The Real Aussie garden consists of a few dried up plants in a variety of different plastic pots. If there are trees they will be palm trees. On the whole, Real Aussies dislike trees almost as much as the Lower Middles.

The shed looks like a real shed — messy to the point of chaos, dirty, comfortable. It is full of girlie mags, grease and apparently useless metal bits and pieces. The main purpose of the shed is to provide a refuge from nagging women, as well as to provide a safe place to keep car tools. It does not hold gardening implements as Kev considers that gardening is women's work.

The lifestyle

This class is heaven for men. All men are Real Aussie by inclination and would like nothing better than to spend their days pottering around their yard (not garden) in black shorts, singlet and rubber thongs. They would love to be able to mess around under the bonnet of their car, to have motorbike bits in the lounge room, a beer whenever they feel like it, and to shout at the missus when she gets out of line.

They envy Kev who spends most of his spare time doing blokey things like fishing, talking about cars and watching races of all kinds — horses, cars, motorbikes, dogs. Kev doesn't take too much notice of Shar but will fall apart if she ever has enough of it all to want to leave. He loves his kids and takes them to the drags, footy, etc, but just as quickly gets sick of their noise and whining and hands them back to their mother to deal with.

Kev considers that men work hard at their manual jobs and ought to be able to relax when they get home. They're not interested in doing things to the house because (a) they're too tired; and (b) they can't see that it matters. Sharon either puts up with the broken door for fifteen years or calls in a tradesman which leads to a first-class row with Kev, who thinks she is trying to piss him off.

Kev thinks it's all bullshit when Sharon complains that women have it tougher than men. Just because she comes home tired from working in the canteen and has to move straight on to the second shift of meals and the washing. Bloody hell, she doesn't work as hard as him during the day. Her mother, Mavis, quickly gave up the struggle to impose gracious living on her menfolk and just put up with it, learning to drink nearly as much as her husband. Sharon still has hopes that Kev will one day grow up.

Food

Kev and Shar eat more takeaway than any other class, especially hamburgers and pizzas. They drink Coke like other people drink tea, coffee or water. When Sharon cooks it is almost always something fried. They don't have set mealtimes but eat whenever they're hungry. If they eat out it will be a pub meal or a café on the way home from the fishing trip. Sharon dreams of going to a fancy restaurant occasionally but Kev thinks they are over-priced rip-offs containing ordinary food and big-headed wankers.

Money

Money is meant to be spent as soon as you earn it. Neither Kev nor Sharon are into saving. 'We're here for a good time, not a long time,' is one of Sharon's favourite sayings. Kev says 'Give the cat another canary,' as he buys his third carton of beer for the week. They always have plenty of cash for a trip to Bali.

Gambling

Kev is the last of the big gamblers. He never reads a book but he will spend hours concentrating on a card game.

He loves the casino and the race track. He will bet on any sport played, or anything else for that matter. Shar likes the pokies, and Mavis has her bingo.

THE DRAG RACE MEETING

Kev and his mates arrive in a hotted-up Monaro which has a boot stacked full of Eskys. All are shouting and singing dirty songs loudly, calling out colourful comments to everyone in sight. They are especially attentive to any girls wearing tight skirts and high heels. When any girl is so ungrateful as to tell them what they can do with their remarks they are highly amused, and keep up the repartee with her for the entire day or until her boyfriend thumps one of them — whichever comes first.

Meanwhile, Sharon has arrived with the other women and kids in a different car — smaller, falling apart. For the rest of the day the women will be able to enjoy themselves by chatting together, supplying food to everyone at regular intervals, and keeping an eye on the kids, while the men get down to the serious business of the day — drinking themselves into a stupor.

Finally, late in the evening, when the children are all exhausted and fighting Sharon's best friend Rhonda is talked into driving the men's car home, which involves stopping at regular intervals to let someone out to be sick.

VARIATIONS

Not all Real Aussies are Australian-born. You can find them speaking Italian or Tagalog or Cockney. Some will be living in housing estates on the outer reaches of any city, and many will be living in the smaller and more run-down country towns. A large number will be living in impressive southern-plantation-style mansions. Instead of trees, they have white plaster lions on the gate and a tradesman's truck in the driveway. Inside these mansions there are two basic styles. One is a cold, bare, white, concrete look. The other is highly ornate — gold every-where, curly carved furniture and thick carpet.

Another variation is the single-storey house which features little shrines and bells near the large wooden front door, several sets of small-sized sandals and a large tiled hall which hides the rest of the house from outsiders.

Whatever their ethnic background, Real Aussies who make a bit of money immediately drop the blue singlet look and go for something much flashier. For a Sunday trip to the country in the 4WD Kev might wear jeans, a short-sleeved shirt, dazzling new trainers, very shiny gold bracelets and a medallion around his neck. Sharon will go in for tight leather jeans, an expensive shirt and more gold jewellery. The children will all have expensive trainers that are three sizes too large, T-shirts and caps with logos.

IF YOU'RE STILL NOT SURE ...

... ask yourself the following questions:

- Do you go to the trots regularly?
- Do you own more stubby holders than wine glasses?

- Do you think any man who spends three hours a week mowing his lawn is an old woman?

- Do you joke that women should be barefoot, pregnant and in the kitchen (but really mean it)?

*   *   *   *   *

If you answer yes to more than one of these, then there's no doubt about your status. If you don't mind being considered a yobbo by the rest of the country then there's no problem. There are advantages to your situation. For example, you will never in your life have to go to dull P&C meetings or waste perfectly good evenings studying for higher qualifications or doing boring community work, as people in other classes feel compelled to do.

Sharon, however, may decide she wants something better. Kev's dream is that he makes a killing at the races, then brings his mates home to enjoy a good feed of prawns and a beer while watching the footy on the enormous new television set. While he's planning the next fishing trip, and describing the boat he intends to buy, the lottery is drawn in the middle of the match and he has won a couple of million. He then buys a large new house and spends the rest of his life having a bloody good time.

As this is extremely unlikely to happen, Sharon pins her hopes on Kev's plastering business doing well. All she asks of life is that they will be able to eventually buy a new house in a new suburb and fill it with new furniture. If she plays her cards right, that is, she keeps Kev happy in bed, she may be able to bring this about.

SHARON TO AARON'S TEACHER

Dear Miss George

I am writting to say I am very unhappy about what happened on Friday at school to Aaron.

I would like you to know Aaron does not punch other kids and anyone who says so is a lier. I think you should be spending less time on music and things like that and know what's happening in the playground under your nose.

Yours sincerely
Mrs Sharon Smith

FOUR

Dot and Brian: Lower Middles

'It'll all come out in the wash.'

The Lower Middle class (also known as 'Respectable Suburbanites), live quiet lives in the suburbs, interested mostly in home and family, and frequently ridiculed in the media — as in Dame Edna Everage. It's OK to have parents who are Lower Middle, even if you consider it best to live a long way away from them, but friends who are Lower Middle are another matter altogether. To be Lower Middle yourself is social death.

SPOTTING THE SUBURBANITE

Many of the younger generation are well aware of their parents' Lower Middle standing and highly embarrassed by their way of life, groaning about having to go back home for the family Christmas. 'God, my parents are so *boring*. They never do *anything*.' Unless of course the children are making it in another class, in which case they will be saying, 'I just love to get back to see Mummy and Daddy. I wish I was able to see them more often.' Not true but it

Dot and Brian debate the merits of liquid versus powder detergent.

makes them sound like caring people with background.

If you are living a Lower Middle life yourself, it can be harder to see it, because in many ways your life is similar to Middle Australia. It's just that everything is on a smaller scale.

The look

Dot

The key word is 'synthetic'. Synthetic clothes keep their shape and colour. You don't have to keep having them dry-cleaned but can keep them immaculate by throwing them in the washing machine or dryer. It seems crazy to

Dot that anyone would want to pay a fortune for something like linen that looks crumpled the minute you put
it on.

Lower Middle women of all ages aim at a very neat
look with their dressing. The word 'prissy' springs to
mind, followed more charitably by 'ladylike'. Dot wears
sandals with stockings. Her mother Gladys still wears a
hat and gloves when she goes to 'town' — that is, the city.
Everything must fit perfectly and, as Dot has a trim figure
(all that housework), she can get away with cheaper
clothes which look hideous in large sizes.

When Dot wears slacks (not pants) they are perfectly clean and ironed; anyway, being synthetic they
always have a knife edge crease down the front. The
Upper Classes can wear sloppy clothes and not drop
caste. Lower Middles can't. Blouses (not shirts) are crisp
and smell of lemon. Dot's underwear takes some
budgeting for, because lots of well-fitting bras and satiny
pants are a must. She and her friends also buy more
petticoats than all the other classes put together.

Older Suburbanite women have an unfortunate
habit of having their hair permed in tight curls, then
adding a waisted polyester dress, cream or bone synthetic open-toed high heeled sandals, stockings, and a
synthetic handbag.

Younger Suburbanite women look smarter, but still
in a neat and somehow sexless way. Dot's daughter Karen
goes to her clerical job wearing a sludge-coloured crepe
suit, a white rayon blouse with embroidery around the
collar, stockings and sandals.

Both Dot and Karen like small, unobtrusive pieces

of gold jewellery, like Upper Middle Caroline's (see Chapter 5, p.55). They can't see how anyone could tell the difference between Caroline's real gold and their imitations.

Brian

Men also wear synthetic and look very spruce. Short-sleeved shirts and tailored shorts with long socks for the office for summer. Before Brian retired as a supervisor, he had begun to wear long trousers to work; the trousers were just slightly too tight, the shirt white nylon. Brian's father wears cardigans with zips or buttons down the front. He never has to buy one because it's a standard birthday and Christmas gift. Nobody knows that he secretly longs for someone to buy him something a bit 'naughty'.

Brian likes grey shoes with a zip at the side. He wears a wedding ring — to stop other women from getting the wrong idea — and a signet ring.

Hair and make-up

Hair is short for both men and women. Brian wears his parted and combed back and to the side, kept neatly in place with hair oil. Women have it cut on a regular basis and set once a week. Despite Dot's general daintiness and preoccupation with hygiene, she doesn't like to wash her hair every day because that tends to make it look messy. Keeping the shape is more important than shine.

Dot buys her make-up from the supermarket where you can get nice cheap lippies and powder.

The Lower Middle house

This may be in a suburb of a large city, but could well be in a country town. Despite the 'Suburban' tag you can find Lower Middles almost anywhere you go.

There are people living a Lower Middle lifestyle in hilltop mansions and in the smaller new houses in outer suburbs. However, the pure Suburban house is the older house in a suburb halfway between the city and the hills or coast or whatever the special attractions of your particular city. It would once have been in a more inner suburb but the Lower Middles have been pushed out of what are now trendy suburbs by either the Upper Middles and Inner-City Sophisticates pushing prices up or by the poor subclass pushing them down.

Dot and Brian have one of the old quarter-acre blocks. The house itself, which they have lived in for the past thirty years, is not all that different from the ocker house or even the poor in its general size and construction. It is, however, neater and cleaner than that of the poor, and much less garish than the Real Aussie's. Its construction material will vary from state to state, but is most likely to be fibro (or asbestos), weatherboard or single brick. In Queensland it will probably be on stilts. Dot and Brian's fence is white picket, but could be almost anything, including low brick or post and wire. There are a few shrubs lining the fence and a neat red-painted concrete path leading to the front door.

Dot and Brian have a tiled roof and a wooden front door with a good solid security screen door obscuring it — to keep out the crims. Both front rooms have single sash windows with sparkling white net curtains.

If you have a chiming doorbell, or one that plays a tune when someone rings, you are almost certainly Lower Middle. Do you have an attractive little decoration near the front door — black plastic palm trees perhaps? A round window containing a nautical scene of some sort? A cheery message on your mat? Does your house have a name — especially 'Dunromin' or 'Emohruo'? An Australian flag waving from the flagpole in the front yard? Lower Middles are obviously proud of their status, or they wouldn't go to so much trouble to announce it.

The garden

Dot and Brian's front garden has a trim lawn with flower beds around the edge, lined with something to stop the lawn from encroaching. Those nifty little pretend rolls of half pine logs are typical; Dot believes that they give an attractive olde-worlde country atmosphere. The flowers will probably be annuals, particularly petunias. Other people might feel exhausted at the thought of putting dozens of flowers in the ground and taking them out a few weeks later, but Brian has plenty of time on his hands, and he can't let the side down as far as the rest of the street is concerned.

Colours are important. Both Dot and Brian like flowers to be as bright as possible and unusual in some way. For instance, their roses have a mauve and white stripe. Shrubs have variegated leaves whenever possible.

There are also the statues to provide interest. Swans, Aboriginals, gnomes — whatever you like. They are made of white concrete or plaster, never natural clay, with features painted in a variety of bright colours.

Dot and Brian have a couple of small trees, but generally speaking Lower Middles don't like trees because they clog drains and gutters and push up paving. Above all, trees drop messy unsightly leaves everywhere and, Dot thinks, if there's one thing that spoils the look of a nice neat lawn it's a pile of decaying leaves. What those Upper Middles see in trees is beyond the Lower Middles. It was a happy day in suburbia when a gadget for vacuuming leaves was invented.

The back garden is what is thought of by other classes as the quintessential Australian fifties backyard. A high fence all around, made of something like asbestos, a small patch of lawn, a path leading up to the Hill's Hoist and a garden shed/workshop. This is smaller than Kev's and doesn't hold car parts — Brian has the Datsun serviced regularly at the local garage. It is for gardening implements and the lawn mower, and is also a refuge where Brian can escape from Dot's housekeeping to do his woodwork or pot his plants. There are shrubs growing against the fences, and more annuals — not in natural clumps but in straight rows.

Inside

Inside, the rooms are small but neat and clean. In Dot and Brian's sixties house the front door opens straight into the lounge room with only a wooden divider screen shielding the room from the door. This has a wooden planter box in front of it. The plants are plastic because Dot can't stand the mess of watering real ones, which only die eventually anyway.

There is a fireplace, but Brian had the wood fire ripped out and a gas fire fitted. They always knew that wood fires were a mistake and now they have been vindicated with councils all over the country banning them because of the damage to the environment. Neither Dot nor Brian have any time for the greenies — loonies, most of them — but they certainly agree with them on this one. The Lower Middle fireplace may be plain brick or a crazy stone pattern.

On the mantelpiece are as many family photos as Dot can fit, especially of all the weddings, plus a few knick-knacks collected over the years while on holidays. She loves the mirror tiles above the mantelpiece, with the picture of a ship etched into them. Three china ducks have been flying across the wall for many years now. Dot was offended when her daughter Clare told her that they are considered such a cliché they were briefly adopted as a joke decoration by the trendies.

When it comes to seating the Lower Middles' motto is 'Comfort is never as important as looks or ease of cleaning.' Dot favours a neat two-seater in an easy-care fabric with antimacassars on the arms (those little lace things), two chairs with pretty covers and a recliner rocker. Even if she had chairs in leather (mock leather, that is), she would cover the arms with something, to prevent staining. There is a coffee table — oblong with splayed legs — and a magazine rack. The standard lamp adds class, Dot feels. Every spare surface is covered with little lace doilies — the pictures and vases all stand on doilies. As well, one of Dot's favourite hobbies is her needlework, so there are embroidered cushions, cross-stitch pictures, and lacy covers on everything in the house from tissue boxes to coat hangers.

The sideboard used to be of pale imitation wood, with glass-fronted doors. However, when Brian retired they treated themselves to some new furniture, and bought some nice modular units in a teak veneer that is so good you can't tell it from the real thing. It holds Dot's collection of glasses plus the bottle of sherry either inside — to keep the dust off it — or in one of the open recesses. However, most of this space is given over to the wedding photos.

In a new house there would be a family room, but Dot and Brian have enclosed the back verandah to make a sunroom/TV room. It's been a godsend. They can use this room almost all the time and the front room can stay looking perfect for visitors.

The carpet goes through the lounge and passage-way, and would go to the dining room if there was one, but not to the bedrooms. The bedroom carpets have a different pattern to match the varying decor of the rooms. The main carpet is of a bright but unspecified pattern — swirling circles of burgundy and brown hide many spills and provide such an interesting touch of colour. As well as the net curtains most rooms have some other 'window treatment' — although not thick draperies which are notorious for collecting dust. Dot likes Venetian blinds but was finally persuaded by Clare to replace them with something more up-to-date.

Bedrooms are all small; the master bedroom will only take a double bed. The dressing table used to be of fifties design, curving blonde wood with a large mirror, but since the retirement it has been changed for modern veneer, also with a large mirror. Dot's mother still has a chenille bedspread but Dot has one of those all-in-one padded bedspreads that go right over the pillows. Pale floral synthetic. Against the pillows is a bride doll holding Dot's nightie.

The other bedrooms have a single bed, small wooden desk and a small bookshelf. Dot and Brian's children have left home but in a young girl's room there would be a collection of soft toys — some of them as big as herself — and in a boy's room cars. Girls would also have ballet trophies filling the bookshelf, and costumes almost overflowing from the wardrobe.

Kitchen

As in any house the kitchen is important. It has lots of cupboards because Dot can't stand leaving things all over benches as some classes do; ockers because they're too lazy to put them away, other classes because they want to show off their hand-painted dishes and copper pots and what have you. The thought of actually eating off things that have been left out for flies to crawl all over is enough to make Dot feel physically ill.

All the same, many Lower Middle homes have a little stand to hang cutlery on (it comes ready fitted with holes in the handles) and a metal container with a handle for drinking glasses, although this last is now optional and becoming harder to find in the shops.

There are many little touches that help to make the Lower Middle home recognisable. For example, Tupperware is important. Everything in the house is spick and span, and what better way to do this than by clever little

Tupperware containers. Dot also performs a real service to Australian industry by the amount of cleaning products she buys. If it wasn't for her and her friends and relations, what would happen to the manufacturers of toilet fresheners, plastic meat covers, etc, etc?

The Lower Middle house feels light and transparent and somehow insubstantial. There's a strong sense that in a high wind it would all blow away. This is partly because it is quite possible that in the whole of the house there isn't one object made of solid wood.

The lifestyle

Family

Dot and Brian are convinced that they are the last of the classes to uphold the old-fashioned family values. This is because most of their time is taken up with keeping the house and garden looking their best, and what social life they have revolves around home and family. Lower Middles are so keen on the importance of family that their children are forced to call all their parents' friends Aunty or Uncle. Likewise, Dot and Brian expect their sons- and daughters-in-law to call them 'Mum' and 'Dad'.

The highlight of the week is Sunday night when everybody goes back to Mum's for tea, which is great fun and nice to know you all still like each other, although it is such a pity Clare lives so far away and hardly ever gets home except for Christmas. On Saturday nights Brian and Dot go to the club for tea.

Dot and Brian spend a lot of their time together, but each has their own separate area of interest as well.

Our Gracious Queen

Female Suburbanites know all about the royal family, and can recite little anecdotes about the doings of the younger royals — you feel they've grown up with your children. Dot sobbed during the funeral. She keeps up to date with the gossip from her supermarket magazines so she can keep up her end of the conversation when she's having her hair cut. Despite her knowledge, Dot talks about 'Princess Di' instead of the Princess of Wales.

Black and Decker man

The Lower Middle man has a busy life. It's not so much the paid job — how much work can you take home when you're a junior clerk? — but it's almost a full-time job writing the letters to the paper, putting up the No Junk Mail sign, keeping an eye on the neighbours' affairs (sometimes literally) and attending rallies protesting about crime, Asians, abortion, and so on. The car needs to be kept shining clean. The lawn takes a lot of work. The house is a never-ending project. Apart from the routine maintenance, there's always another little bit of lattice work or a new blind or birdbath or archway to be installed. Now that Brian has retired there is also bowls three days a week.

Food

Dot and Brian spend a lot of time at the supermarket, keeping an eye on prices, ready to snap up any bargains as they appear. Some people are dedicated enough in this to buy the daily paper solely to go to any store that is offering specials, even if it's on the other side of town. Once they've retired, the Lower Middle couple devote even more time to the daily shopping. Hours can be spent debating the merits of different brands of tinned pineapple.

Food is simple and somewhat old-fashioned. Stews and roasts, sponges, scones and macaroni cheese. Takeaway means fish and chips rather than hamburgers or Chinese. Dot drinks tea rather than coffee. She and Brian have breakfast, morning tea, dinner, afternoon tea and tea at night. Dinner is at twelve, on the dot. Tea is at six. If they give a little party in the evening (that's how Dot collects the Tupperware) they would serve a light supper. Dot is very fond of sweet things and they always have sweets at night, after tea — often tinned fruit and cream. Bread is white, along with flour, sugar and rice. They don't drink a lot but Brian has a beer now and then and Dot a shandy or a nice sweet Moselle.

The table looks very neat. Dot changes the table cloth for every meal, and sets the table neatly, with knife, fork, spoon. Bread plate and knife. The bread is in a Tupperware container and the butter in another. Salt and pepper shakers are also plastic.

Neighbours

Suburbanites know all their neighbours — especially the people on either side. Everyone feels free to call on each other at any time, and is prepared to lend anything from tools to food if asked. One way Brian and his neighbours have got to know each other over the years is because they spend so much time outside in the garden, watering by hand and pottering around.

None of this socialising is in any way formal. The idea is not to go out to dinner with these people, but to form a common bond, a union, as protection against the criminal element who are just waiting to take over the street and against whom they have to be constantly vigilant.

Keeping an eye on neighbourhood happenings is important. Brian joins Neighbourhood Watch, which has the double advantage of helping to ward off crime, and also making him feel like an insider because you get to know such a lot about everyone around you. Not, of course, that it will make any difference in the long run. The good old days are well and truly gone, never to return. The days when you could leave your doors unlocked at night, everyone knew everyone else and these junkies and thugs didn't go around knocking over little old ladies.

The glory box

One expense Lower Middles have to allow for is their daughter's 'glory box'. This is also known as a 'Hope Chest' — for obvious reasons. When she is quite young you buy her a trunk or chest (possibly while on the big trip to Singapore) and gradually she fills it with linen, crockery and cutlery, in readiness for the big day (that is, when she marries).

It solves the question of birthday and Christmas presents for years to come, although it can pose a problem if she wants to live with someone without marrying.

Does she break open the chest, on the understanding that this is as good as it's going to get, or wait for the proposal and the white wedding?

Obviously you hope she will wait, because planning her daughter's wedding is an important activity for the Lower Middle mum. It can keep her occupied for years. Once there is actually an engagement to celebrate the planning slips into top gear.

The wedding

This is the biggest challenge of the Lower Middle mum's life. Can Dot compete with her friends, neighbours and relations? Are her dressmaking skills up to making the bridesmaid's dresses — anywhere between four and eight? (Karen is determined to have the photos in the paper.) Do they have a spare couple of thousand dollars to pay for the photographer? Can Dot stand the thought of making 150 gold-and-white favours for the bridal tables?

Yes, she can and does. Karen and her fiancé help out by saving for twelve months so they can have the photographer they want, and the reception place that Karen has been eyeing for years. She has been sketching wedding dresses since she was a little girl, and had every detail of the wedding worked out long before she met Gary.

Everyone agrees that all the preparation was worth it. From the minute Karen and the girls went off to the hairdressers at seven a.m. until Karen and Gary went around the circle of guests at midnight to say farewell, the whole day was perfect.

Dot cried at the ceremony and during Brian's speech at the reception, especially when he spoke about 'not losing his little girl but gaining a new son'. If it takes them the rest of their lives to pay off it was worthwhile. She could hardly believe what she read in some book about the Upper Middles and Upper Classes liking quiet weddings at home. She nearly burst with pride when the wedding was described in the local paper.

*   *   *   *   *

Being Lower Middle class isn't all bad. While you may not do any actual good for anybody else, neither do you do anyone any harm. It's a stress-free life — easier in many ways than trying to live up to expectations in other classes. On the other hand, perhaps you'd like to hear an interesting conversation before you die.

There are times when Dot and Brian are tempted to throw in the towel and let it all run to seed like the loud family down the street. They never worry, live on the dole, a good life which you're paying for with your taxes.

At other times they feel like moving up. If this is the case, it may not be necessary to move house. As prices soar, Upper Middles are moving into your suburbs and doing up houses in their style — gentrification. You could do the same. Rip out anything made of steel — verandah posts, window frames, front fence, and replace it with wood. Grow as many trees as you can fit onto the block. Burn all your doilies and desist from vacuuming every day.

NEWSPAPER REPORT

Local girl Karen made a beautiful bride when she married Gary last Saturday. Karen looked stunning in a gown of cream satin with a low-cut back and sweetheart neckline. She carried a large bouquet of cream roses and stephanotis. The six bridesmaids were dressed alike in burgundy satin and carried small posies in the same colours as the bride's bouquet. The groomsmen wore dinner jackets with cummerbunds and bow ties to match their partners' frocks.

The bride arrived at the church in a horse-drawn carriage which also conveyed the bride and groom to the reception for 150 which was held at the ever-popular venue The White House. Afterwards, Karen changed into a going-away outfit of cream and burgundy before she and Gary said farewell to their guests. The honeymoon was being spent touring Tasmania.

FIVE

Caroline and Richard: Upper Middles

Alternative names: bloody wankers, snobs,
bloody Volvo drivers, the establishment

ADVANTAGES:

Extremely comfortable lifestyle. Long-lived, because of better nutrition and medical care than some classes, but not as reckless and into fast and dangerous toys as the Seriously Rich.

DISADVANTAGES:

Envy and resentment from other classes. Hard to break into. Money alone isn't enough — you need plenty of confidence and style. May be necessary to ditch many of your old friends and certainly your family. A strain keeping up the image.

* * * * *

This is not necessarily the most desired class in terms of numbers, because it is less noticeable than that of the Seriously Rich, therefore — Q.E.D. — the yobs don't know much about it. However, to those in the know it is

Another moment of family pride for Caroline and Richard

highly attractive. Few newcomers can make it into the ranks of the squattocracy, but anyone can be Upper Middle. It is probably the most secure of all groups. Neither Caroline nor Richard would dream of saying so, but they know that everyone secretly admires them — everyone who matters, that is. After all, they're clever, they've got good taste and although they aren't rolling in money, they aren't exactly starving either.

The look

While many Upper Middle Australians yearn for England, their spiritual home, there are advantages to living in this country and one of them is that you can look good without being branded *nouveau riche*. Even though Caroline would sometimes like to be mistaken for a Sloane Ranger, the English Upper Middles *are* stuck with that boring, dowdy, mismatched look that speaks class but hardly ever looks striking. You wouldn't wear tight jeans or yards of gold jewellery like the rich, but you can wear smart clothes and look both classy *and* attractive.

Caroline

The pure Upper Middle look, though, veers more towards the plain than the showy. Caroline doesn't aim to stand out in a crowd — she prefers to look like everybody else. She wants other Upper Middles to acknowledge her good taste, but isn't concerned if outsiders look at her and think 'dull'. She is aware that most women in the street wouldn't know that her plain dark handbag cost three times as much as their entire outfit, but she knows that her own kind will immediately recognise it, and that's all that matters.

Caroline's whole wardrobe is based on classics. She must have at least one tartan skirt or kilt in a subdued colour — your own family tartan is obviously the ideal. She has either a camel coat or a trench coat styled on the English Burberry, but spends most of her time in blazers. Her favourite is the navy one, because it goes with everything else. Those in colder parts of the country also wear English-style padded jackets, with or without sleeves. Caroline rather likes the look of black, but knows that it is considered slightly tarty, so plays it safe and sticks with navy. The only time she wears black is for evening or very dressy lunches. She has a plain black linen dress, and a similar one in black lace, although with a lower neckline. With either of these she would wear her single strand of pearls.

For everyday wear she has a range of discreet skirts, tailored pants, and jeans. With these she wears plain shirts and the blazers. She has white shirts in silk, cotton and linen, and several white T-shirts. For summer she wears linen dresses with sleeves and collars.

Like Dot, Caroline always looks neat and ladylike. The difference is that all Caroline's clothes are in natural fibres. She is never seen to shop for clothes. They are just there, as though they grew out of her lifestyle. Caroline's mother, being even more secure than Caroline, feels free to wear whatever she likes. Thus a lot of older Upper Middle women get around in messy (but good) clothes, no make-up and straight, short, grey hair — no frizzy perms or blue dye.

Caroline has at least one pair of shoes, probably two or three, with a discreet gold bar across the front. Almost all her shoes will be either navy of different heights and styles, or natural leather loafers or brogues. She has narrow, plain leather belts, a discreet plain watch, sunglasses that are expensive but not rimmed with gold, cashmere scarves and jumpers, and several hats. These aren't anything like the ludicrous circus affairs that the Seriously Rich wear to the Melbourne Cup, although she has one large (navy) one for weddings and the races. Her favourites though are berets and her raffia sun hat. She also owns at least one Hermes scarf.

Her jewellery is old dull gold — expensive but small and discreet.

If Caroline loses anything — sunglasses, a watch — she immediately replaces it with something identical.

Caroline's hair, unlike Nikki's, is dark and she wears it medium length and very neat. It is well cut but simple. She occasionally wears it held back with a band — small, simple, not the fat sausage favoured by the rich — but usually brushes it to one side where it falls naturally in the right places. She wears little make-up, although what she has is of good quality. She spends more on skin-care products than actual cosmetics, trying to counteract the effects of all the hours spent outdoors at the children's sporting events.

Richard

Richard also aims for an expensive but discreet look. Like Caroline, his clothes are all classics in natural fibres. He owns several suits, including one in a dark grey wool, and his own dinner jacket. Upper Middle men wear a suit to work if necessary — top public servants, for instance, always wear suits — but avoid it if they can. For one thing they don't want to look like Mafia hit-men, but mostly they just want to be comfortable and don't have any insecure need to prove anything to anybody.

Most Upper Middle men who have to dress formally for work wear well-cut tailored pants in a plain dark colour, a shirt in a complementary colour — usually a lighter shade of their pants colour — a subtly patterned tie and black or dark brown leather belt and shoes. They would never carry one of those men's handbags. Keys and wallets go in pockets, and mobile phones on their belt. Mobiles aren't flashed around ostentatiously, but used naturally, as a useful everyday device.

Richard runs his computer systems design business from home so mostly wears chinos, a pale blue shirt and brown leather lace-ups. He never wears shoes that zip up the side, and particularly not if they are grey and imitation leather — an expression the Upper Middles consider a gross contradiction in terms. When he has lunch meetings he adds a plain tie and jacket.

This outfit takes him just about anywhere, although he also has a collection of trousers of varying degrees of formality — jeans, Oxford bags, corduroys (but not worn ones). At the beach house he lives in baggy shorts, big polo shirts and jumpers, and leather sandals without socks. In winter he wears oversize hand-knitted thick woollen jumpers or a Husky. He has Ugg boots for the ski lodge, but would never wear them to the supermarket.

His hair is well-cut in a modified version of whatever the current trend is, but basically short back and sides, longer on top. He washes it every day but never blow dries it. Aftershave is light and fresh-smelling.

Sophie

Caroline and Richard's daughter Sophie and her friends are amongst the best-dressed women in the country. Sophie secretly admires her mother's quiet good taste, but adds more dash when it comes to herself — she is still keen to be noticed. She has far more time to devote to herself than her mother does, and enough money to buy the best. She buys brand names, but only in styles suited to her age. Being tall and athletic she looks marvellous in short skirts and skimpy tops, managing to look sexy but not vulgar.

Likewise, her hair could be any colour and style, but will never look tarty like Kylie's. (She knows Kylie from her part-time job at the supermarket.) Sophie has had her ears, nose and belly-button pierced, mostly to irritate Caroline, but stops short of tongue, lips, nipples or anywhere else too intimate or painful.

Nicholas

During his university years, their son Nicholas lives almost entirely in baggy shorts, very large T-shirts and bare feet or leather sandals. His hair is wild. However, because he is tall and well-built and the clothes come from top of the range brands he never ever looks remotely like Kev or Donny. Caroline tries hard to force him into other things, although it is obvious just from looking at him that he is a conservative professional in embryo. However drunk he may get (and he sometimes gets very drunk indeed), he will never wake up in the morning to find that he has a tattoo on his chest.

Getting there

It helps tremendously to be born into this class, but it isn't essential. If you are a woman you can marry into it. If you are a man you can work your way up. You'll need to gain a degree, preferably becoming a professional of some sort. You can also enter through the business world, but you have to be very careful which business you choose. Something vaguely professional-sounding is best. Otherwise there is a real risk that you will end up as Middle Australian or Seriously Rich.

Another method is to save your money carefully, buy a house in the right suburb, and send your children to the best schools. This has its dangers however. You might, for instance, have very shy and unattractive children, whom no one will invite to parties, which will put you at a decided disadvantage. You are also limited to the life-span of your children's schooling. It is possible you will be accepted for a while, but then sink without trace once the children have left school.

Although Upper and Lower Middles have little in common, it is in fact easier to move up from Lower Middle than Real Aussie because your parents are less likely to be loud and embarrassing. They may not shine, but they won't turn up at your parties uninvited to get drunk and tell everyone about your Uncle Dougie's jail term. Middle Australians can make the transition most easily.

You are at a distinct advantage if you move inter-state before you attempt to join this class. You can then write a new version of your previous life. Don't be too inventive, simply learn to be vague about details. Then you can talk about 'a lovely little school' in whatever town you like, without specifying whether government or private school, and hope that nobody in the room comes from that town.

The house

Outside

It is difficult to enter this class without a *certain* amount of money, because the right house in the right suburb is expensive. You can follow the old adage of the worst house in the best street, but it will still set you back a substantial amount.

You can also rent, but it's tricky. Everyone will know the history of every house in the area, and who last bought and sold it for how much. They will know that you're renting, and you will have to have a very good reason for doing so. When you're still on the way up you may live on the outer edge of a desirable area, causing you to be hazy about details when discussing your address. It's worth the aggravation because your children still go to the local school and meet the right children.

House styles vary from state to state — Queenslander, Gothic Revival and so on — but the most typical style is Federation. Basically, you need to buy an older house with wide verandahs and lots of trees in an established 'leafy' (see below) suburb, or just possibly in an older inner-city suburb that has been renovated. You may also live in one of the more attractive large, established, country towns. The house will be brick or stone, either one or two storeys, with several sets of chimneys. The roof can be iron, unobtrusive clay tiles (not blue) or slate. There will be several sets of windows, possibly one or two bay windows.

The door must be substantial — solid wood, possibly with stained glass sections. The verandah floor can be of wood or tiles — an unobtrusive black and white diamond pattern looks good and subconsciously reminds visitors of hallways in grand English country houses.

Once you've bought the right house you will have to spend a substantial amount of money doing it up. The trick is to know what to spend the money on. Above all, you have to resist the temptation to actually neaten the house up in the process. This is crucial. The front, especially, has to look slightly shabby (although not as much so as the Intellectuals' house). The steps, wooden verandah boards and verandah posts should all look original. This is part of making the statement that you don't give a toss about money or status. (You do, obviously, but you can't let on.)

Richard and Caroline don't go in for high fences and elaborate security systems like the Seriously Rich. Simplicity and an apparently low-key style are the aim. They therefore have either a low brick wall or white picket fence — they don't worry about it looking like a Lower Middle picket fence because they know that the different size of the houses, the trees and so on give it a very different feel. They have a recycled brick path, with moss or tiny flowers growing at random among the bricks. There is a lawn on either side of the path, not unlike the Lower Middles, but not as aggressively neat as theirs. Upper Middle people have more important things to think about than the state of health of a patch of grass.

The garden

While the Upper Middle garden will take an immense amount of planning, it must look absolutely natural, as though plants just happened to be in exactly the right place by accident. There must be no natives and no tropical plants whatsoever. Temperate climate trees and bushes are the things to go for, and flowers should be perennials — something substantial like agapanthus that flowers on its own without you having to fuss over it, and fills up the garden with green for the rest of the year.

Roses are important in Caroline's garden. She likes climbers, hedge roses and old-fashioned roses, in pale colours. Off-white, very pale pink, pale lemon and pale apricot are all suitable colours. While you will have to learn all about caring for them you will at the same time have to make sure they retain the blurred, slightly unkempt look of the rest of the garden. A rose bush that looks as though it has been pruned with an electric hedge trimmer is not the aim.

Trees are central to the whole look — indeed to your whole way of life. Not for nothing are your suburbs called the leafy suburbs. Deciduous trees have more good qualities than you can easily list. They are attractive, they provide shade in summer, light in winter, colour in autumn and sometimes in spring as well. You can hang the children's swings from them and build their cubby houses in the wide-spreading branches. Parties and barbecues are a hundred times more sophisticated and enjoyable when held under a large spreading tree.

Trees can hide unattractive features of your house and help to maintain that slight air of mystery. The houses of other classes have no ambiguity about them. Sitting there on their bare and open blocks, the whole house can be seen — you can practically count the number of rooms and know exactly what they would look like. Your house is different. It is more exciting, more interesting — like you. What secrets does it hold? Your house always looks much larger from the inside than the outside, while the Lower Middle and Middle Australian house looks bigger from the outside.

Another thing about trees is that they help to support your fantasy of living in a civilised, northern-hemisphere environment. Shuffling through the autumn leaves feeds Caroline's romantic soul — she could be anywhere in the world — Virginia, London, Paris.

Large maples are a good choice, or beeches or elms, along with liquidambars, silver birches and jacarandas. Chinese tallows have taken off in recent years. White cedars never go out of style, nor camphor laurels. Conifers are fine in pots — especially a pair of them on a verandah. However, tasteful clumps of conifers arranged in the middle of the lawn are Middle Australian.

Caroline also likes to have an unusual tree of some sort, something that is difficult in some way. A silver birch in a hot climate, an avocado in a cold — anything that takes a lot of skill and patience to get flowering, fruiting, growing.

Trees are the main reason that you will need to look for your house in an older suburb. Trees that have been bought at an advanced state and plonked in the garden always look artificial.

Inside

Your adage is 'Old is good'. The great thing about being Upper Middle is that you can have all the benefits of living in a lovely old house, but can also afford to make it comfortable. Intellectuals or the poor subclass may be able to rent older houses, but they have to put up with cold in winter, heat in summer and turn-of-the-century plumbing. Caroline and Richard meanwhile spend thousands having wiring, modern plumbing, heating and cooling systems installed.

More still will be spent on extensions because one of the major drawbacks of older houses is their lack of bedrooms, bathrooms and family rooms. High ceilings, large sitting and dining rooms, most with charming old fireplaces — yes — but modern conveniences no. As Richard and Caroline want extensions to fit in with the character of the original house, we are talking a lot of money.

Having the wooden bay windows made to match the originals costs. So do cork-tiled floors, plaster mouldings, enormous bathrooms and all the other little touches that make the Upper Middle house. Some people may think that it is cheating to want old-style character without all the inconveniences, but you think it is having the best of both worlds. It also gives you something to talk about with the neighbours. Comparing the trials and tribulations of your renovations is one of the main topics of conversation when you run into them at the gourmet food shop on the corner. Your builder should be either marvellous, very creative, the best, or a complete disaster. Appalling mistakes that take a lot of negotiating and fixing are a nuisance in themselves but do provide endless hours of discussion at dinner parties.

The lounge room (drawing room? sitting room?) will be large, with an open fire and large bay windows. If you live in a cold part of the country you can have central heating discreetly tucked away, but the open fire will still be lit whenever you have people around for dinner. There may be a chaise longue in dark green velvet and a couple of ancient tapestry chairs. No one in their right mind would sit on either of these — the chaise longue is too uncomfortable, the chairs too fragile. However, there will also be a much more comfortable large sofa.

The Upper Middles are one of the few classes to use a formal dining room regularly. It is in a traditional colour — Caroline's is dark red, with a family heirloom dining-table. The sideboard holds old silver and china, cut-crystal decanters of sherry, whisky and port, and a bowl of large roses, arranged simply and somewhat unartistically.

Caroline installs a pale carpet throughout the lounge and dining areas, then covers most of it with old and slightly shabby Turkish carpet. Curtains, which are never ever called 'window treatments', should be either plain dark velvet or Sanderson linen in a pattern of large, pale roses.

The rooms will be filled with beautiful and unusual objects from all periods and from all over the world, although 18th Century English will be the dominant theme. The many pictures covering the walls will also be of varied sources, although large, dark, grimy oils will be the most common. Richard has also collected a few unusual originals, reflecting his hobby of restoring antique cars.

The family room will be one of the most pleasant rooms in the house. Unlike the Middle Australian variety, it won't be a heavy-traffic area in the middle of the house, but a large and separate room at the back overlooking the pool, garden or view. It will have hard-wearing but comfortable flooring — terracotta tiles covered in rugs, or a tight-weave carpet. Caroline loves window seats so has one that runs practically all the way around the room, with handy shelving underneath. Comfortable seating and a large oak refectory table mean that this room is used more than any other.

The lifestyle

Upper Middle style is more about way of life than money. You may, for instance, have more assets quietly salted away than some of the Seriously Rich, but you can't splash it around like they do or you risk looking vulgar. Conversely, there are plenty of tradesmen or Middle Australian teachers or managers who have more in the bank than you, but who don't have your style and taste.

Caroline and Richard consider talking about money the height of rudeness, but make very sure that Sophie and Nicholas understand the value of a dollar. Teenagers work part-time — that's how they learn all the old-fashioned values like reliability. Also an encouragement to keep on studying as they realise they don't want to spend the rest of their life in a kitchen or behind a checkout. Grandparents give children money as a start and teach them about investing.

Caroline and Richard share a strong streak of nostalgic yearning for the good old days. However, rather than expressing this by carping about the crime rate (like that boring little man Brian who helps with the garden) the Upper Middles naturally show more style. Most of the expensive editions of the children's classics are bought by you and your friends. Your children all have Bunny-kins plates.

Typical Caroline day

Just make it in time for the recital at Sophie's school. Furious with Richard who promised to be here but has apparently been held up by work. One of her friends has saved her a seat, thank God. The first time she's stopped all day. There was Nicholas to be run to rowing at 5 a.m., her part-time consulting work, visit to parents (N.B. need to phone brother about mother's health), lunch with three old school friends. Cleaning lady wanted to talk for *hours* — could hardly get away.

Music heavenly (so it should be, considering the fees). The girls all look young and beautiful and inno-cent. Must be the uniforms and the lack of make-up. Hard to believe they're the same crowd who were at Emma's party on Saturday night, all looking about twenty-five and most of them drunk or (you suspect) stoned.

Sophie playing beautifully and looking as though butter wouldn't melt. A big smile for everyone, even you. Has obviously got over her foul mood of this morning when she called you a boring bourgeois has-been. Must want some money.

Damn. That pushy Smythe-Moneybags woman looks as though she's going to come over and talk later. Had no intention of inviting her to Richard's 50th, but it's obviously what she's hoping for, and will probably be hopeless and give in.

Ha! Richard has just arrived and is talking to three of your neighbours in a loud stage whisper. Try to catch his eye to shut him up. If he invites them all over for drinks Caroline will personally kill him because she's already cooked three gourmet dinners this week for his business visitors from interstate and this is one night she is planning to have off.

Manage to put neighbours off until tomorrow night. Go out for quick meal at new local café. Everybody there. End up going on to movies with a few friends. Nicholas and Sophie both off to parties. Caroline and Richard to bed late again.

* * * * *

Once comfortably accepted as Upper Middle, few people see any need to change, although if their children happen to marry into the aristocracy so much the better. Otherwise you feel you pretty much have it made. Caroline and Richard enjoy some of Nikki and Mike's parties (see next chapter) — the champagne is always good — but wouldn't have one of the vulgar mansions of the Seriously Rich for anything.

SIX

Nikki and Mike: Seriously Rich

'Money can't buy you happiness but you'll be very comfortable while you're unhappy.'

ADVANTAGES:

Should be obvious. You don't have to worry about the gas bill. Heaps of friends. Freedom to do what you like.

DISADVANTAGES:

Health risks — fast cars, aeroplanes, downhill skiing, overeating, etc tend to kill a certain number of people every year. Also, continual worry over whether you will be invited to THE party.

* * * * *

The hardest part of joining this class is not, as you might expect, actually becoming rich in the first place. The hard part is *looking rich* (rather than a Real Aussie, Lower Middle or Middle Australian who just happens to have a large bank balance), but not *vulgar*. What you want to avoid is the Beverley Hillbillies syndrome — quick money making a fool of itself amongst people with class.

At this moment, Nikki and Mike know that all that striving for success has finally paid off.

Many of the Seriously Rich are trying desperately to seem Upper Class. Without looking desperate or appearing to take the whole thing too seriously that is in fact your aim too. You hope they'll invite you to things and you hope other people (that is, the hoi polloi) will mistake you for aristocracy. You have to be clear in your own mind though, about the reality. The fact is you are not Upper Class. As long as you remember that and just enjoy what your money has to offer you won't go far wrong.

The look

You don't have to be *born* rich to obtain that sleek, smooth, well-fed, confident style that says money; it can be acquired *after* you've got the money. It is instantly recognisable and appears to be a result of freedom from financial worries as much as from being able to afford a good haircut, because it is apparent even in situations where your clothes and other material goods don't give anything away. Once gained it is never lost though bankruptcy, divorce or prison may blot your life.

Nikki

If the thought of paying more for a casual top than your mother would pay for a lounge suite is frightening, then you aren't ready to do this. If it excites you, you are obviously a natural. Nikki learned the brand names simply by walking around the shops in her area. Escada, Louis Ferard, Frank Usher, Bruno Magli shoes. It's easier today than it was years ago, because many of the labels are on the outside so nobody is in any doubt that it is Gucci or Hermes. After a while it will become second nature; the prices seem normal and Nikki doesn't even realise that she is paying ten times more for her clothes than other women.

Crisp navy and white linen, black velvet headbands, gold on everything, especially sunglasses. (You enjoy the symbolism of it.) T-shirts are always trimmed with gold. Silk, brocade, heavy cotton, bright colours. As she doesn't work, Nikki wears more dresses and less suits than other classes. When she does wear a suit, perhaps for lunch or a wedding, it is something pretty and sexy that couldn't possibly be mistaken for office wear — perhaps in pale pink raw silk. A typical casual outfit is white slacks, flat gold shoes, and a tunic top with a blue and gold yachting motif.

Shoes don't have to be as plain and boring as those worn by the Upper Middles. High strappy sandals (not unlike Sharon's, although obviously costing a lot more) and two-toned shoes are acceptable. The difference between Caroline and Nikki's style of dressing can be summed up in two words — painted toenails.

Nikki is keen to look elegant but has to curb her tendency to buy everything in sight. Shop assistants can be so unscrupulous — they will sell her anything just because she can afford it. And with all that time and money on her hands it is tempting to buy three of everything, whether the colours suit her or not. It's also hard to stick to plain styles and classic designs. When you're paying hundreds of dollars for a pair of jeans you really do want a bit of decoration on them so they don't go unnoticed. Why wear a boring little black dress to a ball when you can afford Swiss cotton lace?

However, while Nikki never stops enjoying the spending of Mike's money, she does tone it down a bit as the years go on. She's worried that complicated hair and all the jewellery at eight o'clock in the morning might look nouveau. Still, she can never resist a new diamond.

It's an odd thing, but the proportion of blonde women is much higher in rich areas than in ordinary suburbs. It's not clear if this is just because rich men marry blondes, or whether they become blonde after-wards, but you will stick out like a sore thumb if you don't do the same. Nikki's is shortish, layered and bouffant with a fringe. It might look tousled at times but never badly cut.

It's years since Nikki has been seen without make-up but she obviously looks after her skin, which is always smooth, matte and powdered. Anyone looking at her can tell immediately that her make-up is one of the more expensive brands. She always smells delicious. Nikki never, ever buys her make-up from the local chemist. Pharmacies are for health foods and sleeping tablets.

Nothing brands you as Lower Class more quickly than dirty, broken, crooked or missing teeth. Nikki had her bridgework done years ago, before she joined the airline. She might never have met Mike otherwise. Luckily she hasn't needed plastic surgery, although her best friend Suzi has had heaps. Nikki is afraid that Suzi is becoming hooked on it, and while Suzi argues that it's really no different to buying new clothes to help her to look good, Nikki recently pointed out to her that it is just a little more dangerous.

Keeping in shape takes up much of Nikki's time. Remember the Duchess of Windsor who said that you could never be too rich or too thin. Swimming, walking, aerobics, skiing — yes, but you may need more. A personal trainer is handy. Nikki knows that it's not so much that they tell her anything new but that having to keep her appointments with them forces her to keep up the exercise regime. As well, the tan needs to be worked at.

Mike

Men also need to be well-groomed, and once you've got money it's all so much easier. A good hair cut does wonders for your looks, but a fit body does even more. Mike has less time than Nikki to work out but there is the home gym, the lap pool, the squash game and the skiing. Keeping in shape could become an absorbing hobby. Anyway, he figures he has to keep trim or it's all something of a waste. He doesn't want to be one of those middle-aged men with fat belly and balding head driving around in a convertible trying to attract the attention of spunky young women.

While he would keep quiet about it, Mike is also prepared to pay for any dental work or plastic surgery that might be beneficial. He blow dries his hair every morning — Richard Boring Upper Middle wouldn't, but why not take advantage of what technology has to offer?

As to clothes, Mike tries to follow Nikki's advice and keep it simple, within limits. Having spent years working hard when he was young he enjoys being able to wear expensive clothes — he will never wear a pair of torn black shorts again — but he is aware that monogrammed shirts are vulgar. He wears suits more than Richard because he feels that while grey suits and silk shirts might be predictable they never fail to look good, especially when made by a good tailor. He has discovered that women are always turned on by a man in a well-cut dinner jacket although not if it is worn with a frilly coloured shirt. In the early days he once, through a misunderstanding, wore a dinner suit to a casual party and it's a mistake he won't repeat. It took years to overcome the neighbourhood's impression that he was a parvenu.

One of the joys of being Seriously Rich is that you are in a position to buy good quality casual clothes; Mike knows he looks fantastic at the yacht club in his non-slip shoes, crumpled pants and white V-necked jumper. His favourite item in his wardrobe though, is his Rolex watch.

Becoming rich

Mike

When you are younger you can get by with a bit of faking — lots of gold jewellery and driving European cars is enough. The rented car, your weekly wage (however small) kept in your wallet to flash around conspicuously in bars, a discreet address that no one is ever invited back to. As you get older it's a different matter. You can't pretend when it comes to the house, the school fees, the boat, the holidays. You need serious money behind you.

You can be lucky — win Lotto, buy the right shares by a sheer fluke, have a great-aunt die and leave you a pile. You could do something slightly (or very) outside the law. Call yourself an importer. What are you buying and selling? Who knows? Do they need to know? In the eighties you could do it all on other people's money but that avenue has been largely closed down.

Or you could do it the hard way, like Mike. He started out as a brickie's labourer and ended up, many years later, owning a highly successful building company.

Nikki

On the surface it appears to be easier for women, or at least the beautiful ones. You simply find some up-and-coming man and marry him, then settle down to a life of ease and luxury with no further effort on your part. It goes without saying that nothing is ever that easy.

For one thing the man who will be Seriously Rich in his forties may be very ordinary-looking indeed in his twenties and easily missed. When Nikki was young and determined to marry a rich man the chap toiling away in the scrapyard down the street didn't immediately spring to mind as the person to provide her with the goodies. She could kick herself now when she meets him at parties with his rather attractive wife who began as a mousy little nobody who helped him with his bookwork.

Of course she loves Mike, but by the time she met him he also had an ex-wife and three children as well as the money. She manages to forget the children for much of the time but suspects there will be a bun-fight over the will; always provided she manages to hold on to Mike until he dies.

As he is in a position to marry just about anybody, it takes talent to steer a rich man to the altar. You have to cultivate a persona that is witty, confident and articulate, but at the same time cool and aloof and hard to get. You do not, contrary to popular belief, dive into bed with him at the first opportunity but keep him guessing for as long as possible. Given that he may well have been too busy becoming rich to be any good in bed this won't be any great hardship.

The hard way

Women can meet their man through work. It isn't necessary to embark on a serious career which you wouldn't want to give up afterwards, but something like air hostessing where you get to look poised and well-groomed while coming in contact with the rich and powerful. Nikki met Mike when she looked after him on a flight to Hong Kong. Acting (TV) and modelling are other good reliable standbys that bring you into the orbit of your target.

It is not unknown for nannies and housekeepers to land their employer as a husband, although if you attempt this you must follow the rules even more strictly than anybody else. You must be extremely beautiful and at the same time hold off sleeping with him for longer than ever.

Other jobs will do, at a pinch. Real estate is good, and public relations. Even clerical skills can be useful provided you only work for firms that contain a high proportion of high-flyers. Whatever your field, make your job into something more important than it ever was before and always look 100% fantastic every day. Today might be the day when you meet your fate. When you're at a party be vague about where you work if you're still on the way up. 'I'm with XYZ,' rather than, 'I'm a data processor at XYZ.'

It's a waste of time to put serious effort into your work because once you're married your rich husband won't tolerate you having a proper job — helping in your friend's flower shop is OK, but nothing that is going to take your attention off him.

The house

Outside

The word is 'big'. Everybody who's Seriously Rich needs a big house. Whenever it's described in the newspapers, which is often, Mike and Nikki's house will be described as 'the luxury home of …' It must be in a prominent position — on the top of the hill, overlooking the river, harbour, lake, or whatever. Even more importantly it must be in a very expensive area. The most wonderful house in the world will look nothing and be worth nothing if it's stuck in the middle of a cheap suburb. You also want to avoid those newer estates full of mock Tudor, mock Tuscan, mock everything houses. You want to be mixing with the really rich, not double-income Middle Australian families hoping to gain in importance through knowing you.

Even when you're in the right street in the right suburb it is easy to make an expensive and conspicuous mistake with the style of the house. Forget those cubist things that look like a child has been let loose with the Lego — a large number of concrete blocks all stacked on top of each other in a variety of patterns, painted white, pink or bright blue, complemented by acres of dark glass.

What you do want is something classical looking. It doesn't have to be really old because you can afford aged materials and mature trees which will soon give it that mellowed appearance. A large two-storey Georgian sandstone mansion would be perfect, or a copy of an early Australian, two-storey squatter's homestead, like the Lintons' house in the Billabong books. Or a Scarlett O'Hara ante-bellum mansion, a French chateau, or an English stately home. Any one of these would make the point that you are a cut above the ordinary.

The garden

Whatever the style of the house, the garden (grounds) will be extremely large and protected by a security fence. The question is, do you make the fence see-through, to show off the splendour, or high and blank, to protect your privacy? Generally speaking, you will go for see-through. After all, the place is big enough so that nobody can actually see into the rooms, and more often than not you won't be there anyway, but in New York or London.

The tasteful rich garden has a beautiful lawn, trees and shrubs, but just manages to avoid that over-groomed, too-careful sheen of the vulgar rich house. Nobody would expect Mike and Nikki to have their place looking as shabby as the Upper Middle house and garden but a touch of faded splendour is just right.

You have to be careful when planning the outdoor lighting. The possibilities are almost limitless these days. The garden shouldn't be lit up like a Christmas tree with every tree and bush floodlit, but a little bit of light-hearted showmanship is acceptable. Mike and Nikki have one significant tree backlit, and ground lights along the driveway. Security lighting of course. However, while it's fun, fog wafting amongst the trees is over the top.

While you will be able to afford a landscape designer and gardener, you will have to be prepared to rein them in. They probably wouldn't make the fundamental mistakes that Mike and Nikki might if left to their own devices, such as plonking a dozen palm trees in a straight row in front of an older-style house, but they may be inclined to an over-ordered look. You do not need thirty lavender bushes all of exactly the same shape and height, nor a planting of roses featuring alternate bushes of cream and white.

There's no need to be too modest about it all — what's the point of being rich if you feel hesitant about enhancing the garden with a swimming-pool, tennis court and outdoor entertainment area? The word, though, is 'functional'. You can have anything as long as you show there's a use for it. A tennis court that has never been played on looks ostentatious; one that is used regularly helps to make your whole house and garden look Upper Middle, even Upper.

A striped canvas awning is sensible in our climate; classical columns holding up nothing in particular look ridiculous, and so on.

Inside

Nikki brought in an interior decorator because she wanted to have something to talk about at dinner parties. Others make a personal crusade of tackling it themselves. Doing up an entire house from scratch takes nerve. It's so easy to get it wrong. On the other hand you may want a say in the decoration of the house that you are going to be living in. Like chefs, designers have definite ideas about what they do and don't like and they're not all that keen on anything classic, like the English country-house look which they consider done to death. The Uppers and Upper Middles, on the other hand, can't see past this style.

If you're doing it yourself the choice is antiques or modern, depending on the style of the house. Both have traps for the newcomer so study the magazines, shops and your friends' houses very thoroughly before you start spending. Modern is possibly the hardest because you can so easily end up with something that looks like a factory, although this may change once stainless steel has had its day. A beautiful antique piece will go in any setting but you can't stick a lone modern object in the middle of a traditional room and know for sure that it will work.

Marble and leather, glass, enormous modern paintings and fantastically expensive pieces of modern sculpture are part of the look. You can also have every piece of technology ever invented.

Floral decorations: a few pink carnations slowly dying in a small cut-glass vase is not the idea. The large-leafed, primary-coloured look is taking a long time to die, so you wouldn't go wrong with that. If in doubt, study the flowers in your nearest café or homeware shop.

Tips: The most extreme styles date the most quickly. Anything in leopard skin is probably a mistake.

The lifestyle

Money

Initially you may find it hard to start spending money. Having started life without any, you can't get over the fear that tomorrow it will all be gone. This is one of the big differences between you and the Upper Classes. However broke they may be, they always think of themselves as naturally rich, and believe their present poverty is only an unfortunate temporary state.

Once you start spending, though, it can be even harder to stop. You have to be firm with yourself. A limited budget does wonders for your taste, forcing you to think about every purchase and therefore working out whether it suits you, is suitable, etc.

Social life

One of the main points of being Seriously Rich is that you are the kid with the ball. Like the shy fat boy in the school playground who can't get anybody to play with him until he brings along the football, you easily attract people around you if you have money. They will be falling over themselves to be invited to your parties, to sail on your yacht, to stay at your holiday house.

These hangers-on have their place in making you feel important, but what you really want is to be invited to other rich people's parties. It isn't your money that gets you on the invite list, but your wit and presence — there are plenty of rich people sitting at home alone in their mansions wondering why nobody asks them anywhere. Much of it comes down to your background. Those who started out as Real Aussies are more likely to be successful than those with Lower Middle origins, because the Lower Middles find it impossible to let go, stop saving their money for a rainy day and just have a damned good time.

Nikki takes part in the fund-raising round, helping to organise balls, dinners and arts performances for some worthy cause. She learns the ropes by offering to help friends with something they are organising, rather than jumping in at the deep end and having a disaster on her hands. Once you go to enough of these things, and gain a reputation for working hard ('tirelessly' is the word), you will eventually be accepted, as long as you have wit, confidence, looks and style. Luckily, character as such doesn't enter into it.

Getting your photo into the social pages is essential. This is another of the many differences between the Seriously Rich and the Upper Middles. They will be attending some of the same functions as you (the more arty ones), but nobody knows they're there because they avoid the cameras. Just as well, probably, seeing Nikki's diamonds and blonde mane are more photogenic than Caroline's pearls and mousy hair, but their snooty wish to stay out of the limelight is one of the many things that annoys you about them. However, you need the publicity and thank God daily for the invention of the camera, which means you have a chance to become known.

Your motto — If you're not in the VIP tent, it's not an event worth attending.

Tips for new players

If you're not sure about things like which knife and fork to use, then buy a good etiquette book and study the pictures. E.g. always break your bread and rolls by hand, never with a knife. Always use a butter knife and jam spoon. The biggest mistake of all is to start stacking up the plates at the end of a restaurant meal.

Best avoided

- Stretch limousines.
- Champagne and caviar all the time.

- Telling people how much your house/car/boat/ furniture/jewellery/plastic surgery cost.

- Try to avoid showing off in general. There's something about complaining about your housekeeper that sounds particularly *nouveau riche*. The Upper Middles shut up about their cleaning ladies and pretend they do it all themselves.

The 21st

When Peachie turns 21 Nikki decides it's time to consolidate the family's leading social position by pulling out all the stops and throwing the party of the year. *Everybody* is invited and all but the most snooty turn up. Caroline has been telling everyone what a bore it will be, but can't resist going.

Peachie and Nikki look fabulous in dresses that complement each other — Peachie's is tighter and she doesn't need a bra, and her blonde hair is long and straight, unlike her mother's elaborate coiffure, but it is almost true that, as everyone keeps saying, 'they could almost be sisters'. Mike looks debonair in a new dinner jacket. (He still has to remember not to call it a tuxedo.)

Two gardeners have worked night and day for months to have the grounds at their best. The marquee is spectacularly decorated and the fireworks over the water can be enjoyed by the entire city. The champagne is the best, the food delicious. Everything — the ice sculpture, the ropes of flowers, the food, the five-tiered cake — is in pink, Peachie's favourite colour.

Reporters from various media are out in force, but to Nikki's relief are stopped by their editors from printing the photos of Mike with his hand on Suzi's bottom, or Rudi being sick into a rose bush. There is a funny smell in the air which Nikki doesn't think can be totally accounted for by the many cigars being smoked, but Peachie assures her that none of her friends would dream of bringing along illegal substances.

Nikki enjoys the night on the whole, although she wonders what on earth they can do to top it, when Peachie finally decides to get married.

* * * * *

Despite the fact that most of the population wish to be like you — hence all those Lotto tickets — you have your traumas just like ordinary folks. Children are always a worry. Despite everything you've done for them they often end up rejecting your whole way of life — although they don't leave home until they are twenty-five. Nor are marital relations easy. All those beautiful men and women, all that temptation, all that lovely freedom. It's hard not to feel as though you have a *right* to have affairs.

If it all seems too much, you could chuck it and become Upper Middle, or even Middle. But whenever you're tempted to feel too sorry for yourself, try to remember back to what it was like when you were young, had no money and had to catch buses everywhere.

SEVEN

Virginia and Wolfgang: Intellectuals

Putting your brains to good use — by being an Intellectual

ADVANTAGES:

Lifestyle not unlike Upper Middle. Good wine, books, music. Interesting conversation.

DISADVANTAGES:

Tiring. You can't ever let up complaining about the government/the rich/the stupid and so on.

*   *   *   *   *

Intellectuals are always grumpy. For one thing, life is too serious for them to be light-hearted. All those people dying of AIDS, the environment falling apart before our eyes, overpopulation, the Americans, the arms race. The miseries of the world are on their shoulders. This would be admirable except that what they are really furious about is that they themselves are living a comfortable Middle Class life in a peaceful democratic country.

Being an Intellectual has little to do with being intelligent. As with other classes, it's about a choice of lifestyle. There are plenty of perfectly clever, educated people who gain their degrees and go out to make a difference in the world who will never be considered Intellectuals because they choose not to follow the lead of the self-appointed arbiters of ideas.

The look

Wolfgang

This is one of the few classes where the men generally look better than the women. Corduroy pants and good quality shirts (check or denim, and crumpled looking) tend to suit most men. A beard is compulsory and Wolfgang wears glasses whether he needs them or not. Hair should be long and tied back, but *not* in that oily way of the Italian nightclub owner. Being drier and light-coloured, it looks quite different. For casual wear cotton harem pants with a loose cotton top.

Wolfgang does not own a suit and never ever wears one. For something like a wedding he would wear either a jerkin or a heavy linen shirt with a loose jacket or cotton waistcoat. If the invitation said evening dress he would refuse to attend. Because everything is of natural fibres and loose-fitting, all men, even the small ones, look solid and sexy and at the same time dependable and confident.

Virginia

The best thing about Virginia's look is her jewellery — lots of silver rings on slim brown fingers. On the other

Even if it takes another six bottles of wine, Wolfgang and Virginia are going to come up with an original name for this baby.

hand there are few women over thirty who look really good with long straight hair, no make-up, loose cotton skirts and dresses, hairy legs and flat natural leather sandals. Everybody else has thrown their seventies shawls into a trunk and their children use them for dress-ups, but Virginia is still wearing hers. She has to make up for all this by being very interesting and intelligent indeed, and bloody good in bed. Otherwise there's a danger that Wolfgang might one day run off with a younger Intellectual.

One of the reasons Intellectuals like to find a university teaching position is not only so they can have plenty of time for their private research, but so they can wear whatever they like. If Virginia was offered a job anywhere else she might be expected to wear high heels and make-up, which could lead to a major crisis of conscience.

If Intellectual women do have to dress conservatively for work, they adopt a no-nonsense dark suit look. It's an odd thing that the more radical the feminism the more masculine the clothes. Dark pants, short spiky hair and waistcoats are essentials; the only concession being the long dangly earrings.

BECOMING INTELLECTUAL

It's pointless to consider joining this class unless you are 'liberal' — that is, you don't vote for the Liberal Party. Conservative Intellectuals have it tough.

Becoming an Intellectual is a sensible option for the cleverer children of the Lower Middle or poor, who naturally don't want to live their parents' lifestyle but aren't yet ready to reject their background, because it seems either ungrateful or politically incorrect to do so. To be Upper Middle or Seriously Rich is ostentatious. To be Intellectual is acceptable.

The other recruiting ground is the young of the Middle and Upper Middle Classes. They will almost certainly settle one day into a lifestyle very like their parents, but not yet. Young rich people may live as Intellectuals for a short time but it's more of a whim than a settled conviction, and the lack of creature comforts will tell before very long.

The easiest way to gain a foothold in this class is to enrol as a university student, preferably in an arts course of some kind. Geography or financial management means you will do it harder, and perhaps never really belong.

The house

Outside

When they are younger, Wolfgang and Virginia rent a house. It has to be in a 'good' suburb, but somewhat run-down or they wouldn't be able to afford it. Generally, this means an older stone or brick house in a suburb that is on the verge of being bought up by the Upper Middles. If possible, it will be within reach of the university. The idea of buying an affordable house in an outer suburb is, of course, anathema. Intellectuals must have high ceilings, polished floorboards and interesting and congenial neighbours who aren't going to spend every five minutes mowing their lawns. (None of them have any lawns — they're too busy doing more important things, like saving the world.) They also need access to public transport and the right shops. Plastic supermarkets are not for them. They need small, individual shops and fresh-food markets.

If you're in any way 'arty' it is also possible to live in a hills suburb, or other country area where painters, writers and performing artists congregate, which may be cheaper, provided you get in fairly early before the enclave is discovered by the hobby farmers.

Inside

The house has few modern amenities, but a certain whimsical charm from the large rooms and open fireplaces with original mantels and surrounds. Uncovered floorboards are the ideal but if there is carpet Wolfgang and Virginia cover it with matting to avoid having to look at the hideous colours chosen by the bourgeois family who owned the place in the fifties. Although they would hate to live in the tropics — all that heat cooks your brains — a temperate climate is a plus because the house is freezing in winter.

In the living room they have a few very good pieces of furniture in something solid like mahogany, and an enormous, shabby and comfortable couch. There is little or no attempt at obvious decoration. Everything has to look as though it is there for a good reason and has been there forever. If they're from a poorer background they won't have any form of decoration except posters on the walls — advertising either rallies or arts festivals. There may also be prints of their favourite writers and philosophers. If they're from Upper Middle there will be a few more things scattered here and there. Having been brought up with silver and antiques, Virginia and Wolfgang don't even realise how valuable they are until the unemployed poet whom they are giving shelter to makes off with them one night, headed for a pawnshop.

In the seventies Virginia would have had enormous paper flowers and bits and pieces made from string hanging around. The modern Intellectual is terrified of making any overt statement about his or her alternate lifestyle. They want it to be obvious without having to be spelled out. The main physical indicator of Wolfgang and Virginia's taste is their books and music collection. The sound system must be first class, although not ostentatious, while the collection of CDs will be enormous. (See 'Aussies do IT', p.183.) Every room in the Intellectual's house will have at least one bookcase, probably more. The books won't be arranged in neat rows and regularly dusted, but will be all over the place, standing up and lying down, each shelf doing double duty.

The kitchen is an original, in that everything is in its original state. The Upper Middles strive hard to achieve a look like this, with scrubbed wood tables and bunches of dried herbs hanging here and there. The difference is that they have discreet heating and cooling systems tucked away, a dishwasher and a fantastic four-oven system, while Virginia really is trying to cook on the old wood stove.

The dining room will generally be covered in books and papers and may be where Virginia keeps the computer, but it will also have a very large table for entertaining. The table will be solid wood, and will never see a table cloth. There may be ethnic table mats of some kind. Serving platters will be large, brightly coloured pottery. Cutlery will be silver, but not the same as that used by the Uppers or Middles. It will be heavier and plainer. Glasses will also be very heavy glass or pewter.

The main bedroom will have an extremely large bed, possibly a water bed. Wolfgang and Virginia's few Middle Class friends are pruriently curious to know what sex is like on a water bed. There may also be a large solid chest of drawers, but not much else. There certainly won't be any artful arrangement of furniture, antiques and pictures, as in the Upper Middle house. However, the bookshelves will be overflowing.

There will not be a family room in the suburban sense, although there may be a room in the middle of the house that gets used as family room, with a TV and a comfortable couch. There will be one bathroom, and several minor bedrooms. The laundry will be at the back of the house and not very nice. Ditto for the one bathroom.

The Intellectual's house can look unbelievably messy. In fact, it's an essential part of the image. At first glance it's hard to tell the difference between this mess and that of the Real Aussies', but they are fundamentally different. Wolfgang and Virginia's mess consists mostly of newspapers, books, research papers, empty wine bottles and children's toys. Real Aussies have food scraps and beer cans, car parts; practically anything but books.

The apparently chance look of the Intellectual house is, it hardly needs to be said, an illusion. Look carefully and you will see that there are no biographies of right-wing politicians, no recordings of light popular music, no plastic objects of any kind (and not just because they're bad for the environment).

The lifestyle

Sex and its consequences

Despite all the hairy armpits, sex is a major preoccupation of the Intellectual. Wolfgang and Virginia used to go in for free marriage, so Virginia didn't feel left out when Wolf was having affairs, but it didn't work very well. Jealousy may be a suburban emotion, but they were surprised at what a painful one it could be. However, they still have more affairs than any other class except the Seriously Rich, and Wolfgang in particular is always open to suggestion. He would never lower himself by being seen with anybody Upper Middle or Seriously Rich, however attractive she may look, but young, thin and pretty Intellectual women are another matter altogether and an ever-present hazard to Virginia.

She believes in freedom of the individual and all that, of course, but when you get right down to it, it's a major bore to find yourself left alone to bring up the kids. Especially when those kids are noisy, dirty, self-opinionated little charmers who have always been allowed to express themselves in whatever way they like, which tends to mean staying up until midnight and hogging the conversation when their parents have guests.

They also tear around like maniacs in public places, looking and sounding surprisingly like Real Aussie kids. The difference is that while the Real Aussie parent can give them a good whack, Virginia feels obliged to have a reasoned talk with them, which takes a lot longer and is far less effective. Onlookers will be fairly divided in their opinions about this. About half will be tsk tsking at the smackers, while the other half will be shaking their heads over Virginia's apparent incompetence. 'That child needs a good smack.'

Money

Wolfgang and Virginia have one major hurdle to overcome in regard to money. They have a hatred of any
talk about the subject; it simply shouldn't dictate anything about life. Unfortunately, their tastes are very
similar to the Upper Middles — good wine, good food,
books, music, plays, travel, etc — which don't come
cheap but, unlike the Upper Middles, they don't have a
large income. However, Intellectuals always find money
for what they consider to be the essentials of life. Not
having a car, paying off a mortgage or spending money
on boring things like bathroom cleansers (bad for the
environment anyway) or power tools helps.

Travel

Despite the lack of ready cash, travel is a must (see
'Getaway', p.200.) When Intellectuals get home they don't
tell everyone about the appalling airline journeys, nor
the twenty-hour train ride with the suspect food that
gave them the runs for the next four weeks. They are
above thinking about such things — they just arrived,
almost spiritually. But they do wax lyrical about the
beauty of the people and their way of life and what they
discovered about themselves. Above all, travel is a good
starting point from which to attack everything about the
way of life in Australia.

Virginia and Wolfgang are disgusted by all the
Aussies who go flocking to Bali without worrying too
much about Indonesian politics. Wolfgang suspects most
of them don't even realise they are in Indonesia.

Politics

Politics is something that other people think about once every few years when an election comes around. To Virginia and Wolfgang it is as much a part of them as breathing. They never do anything in isolation. Everything they eat, wear, read or listen to has a deeper significance. Watching the TV news is almost a health risk — both Virginia and Wolfgang become so incensed at what the government is doing that they can hardly sleep.

If Virginia hears an acquaintance joking about her lazy husband she feels an obligation to lecture the woman for three hours about women's rights. If their children's school tries to introduce religious instruction they will start a protest group — comparative religion, yes, but Christianity alone is a no no. If a nuclear powered ship tries to enter their city they are out there in a dinghy.

Bland conversations about nothing are not for the Intellectual. No reactionary opinion can go unchallenged, no light chitchat be tolerated. Virginia and Wolfgang generally prefer to mix with their own kind, because they are so appalled by the selfishness and sheer ignorance of everybody else. Even if they believed in Christmas, they would avoid going home for the festivities because of Uncle George's fondness for the Liberal Party.

New Age

Virginia is on a constant quest to improve the quality of life for herself, Wolfgang and everybody else in the universe. We are, after all, all part of the same cycle of creation. She has tried everything herself — Buddhism, crystals, rebirthing, aromatherapy — and is delighted to see that people from all walks of life are beginning to see the light. Her sister Barbara wonders how anybody so intelligent can be so gullible and occasionally implies that Virginia has taken leave of her senses. However, Virginia triumphantly notes that Barb has herself begun to meditate on a regular basis.

Food

Intellectuals have a problem with food. It is an important aspect of the image and they must get it right, but it places them in something of a bind. Naturally they don't want to be anything remotely like the Lower Middles, swapping sponge recipes. Nor do they want to buy hamburgers every night, like the Real Aussies, because it's all too American. Wolfgang ostentatiously boycotts McDonald's because of all the trees cut down to feed the cattle to fill the hamburgers. They can't afford to eat out all the time, and in any case Virginia has vague, jumbled ideas of Bloomsbury, French provincial cooking, self-sufficiency. It seems somehow noble to cook for yourself. It's just a pity it's so time-consuming.

Vegans and vegetarians don't find it a problem because their diet is a cause in itself. Even though it takes up a great deal of their time, it's time well spent because it provides such a good chance to harangue people about their eating habits. If invited to a meal they don't just discreetly put the meat to one side, but make a point of explaining their beliefs to all. Surprisingly, most meat-eaters are quite good-natured about catering for them, even though they know that when they are invited to a vegetarian's home the favour won't be returned.

Intellectuals drink a lot, especially good red wine. When hitching around Europe in their early student days they drank wine that could run a car, but now they've settled down it has to be decent stuff. This is just as well because when they have people for a meal the food might be ready by midnight and it might not and their guests need some nourishment to keep them alive. Either Virginia or Wolfgang will be busy with the cooking — takeaway gourmet is a cop-out — but they don't want to miss any of the conversation, so if a good argument gets going the food has to wait. They obviously wouldn't be caught dead doing anything as Middle Class as giving dinner parties, but inviting people around to eat, drink and talk half the night is their favourite form of entertainment.

As well, they are keen on café life; sitting over a coffee and watching the world go past is so reminiscent of Europe. The changes to Australia's laws allowing food and drink to be served at outside tables is the single most important reason why Australian Intellectuals are now reconciled to living in this country and don't go flocking overseas at the rate they did in previous decades.

* * * * *

As they get older, Intellectuals face a choice: continue with their present lifestyle with the risk of ending up as sad, ageing hippies, or become Upper Middle and risk charges of selling out. Most will in fact settle into a form of Upper Middle . When their parents die and leave them some cash, Virginia and Wolfgang will finally buy a house. It will be furnished simply but expensively. There will be a resemblance to the standard Upper Middle house, but with important differences. The Intellectual will have polished boards instead of the Upper Middle carpet; ethnic furnishings and decorations rather than English country roses. But both share an atmosphere that is somehow reassuring. This is how it's meant to be.

Some people remain Intellectuals all their lives. It's a wonderful class for anybody who wants to escape from real life and ordinary people.

FROM VIRGINIA'S DIARY

Oh God, I am sure that Wolfgang is on the verge of another affair. On Saturday night he spent hours talking to Pandora about her new book and pretending to be fascinated. I wonder if he knows that I heard that pathetic joke he made about Pandora's box. The thing is, I know that he believes writing biographies of retired politicians is a sell-out, especially Liberal politicians. How can he do it? She sat there the whole time looking all innocent and serene, although I noticed that she couldn't look me in the eye. Does she think I'm stupid? Does he?

I know I should leave. I know I should, for my own self-esteem. Why do I feel so bound to him? Oh God, I can't bear to go through all that again. The lies and bullshit. All the late nights when he'll say that he has extra classes. The sex every night — he seems to think that making love to me can somehow make it all right that he's also making love to somebody else.

Perhaps there's some point to all this pain. Not, of course, in the Judaic-Christian religious sense of there being a higher plan for everything, but maybe one day I will be able to turn it to some good use by writing about it. Nobody has yet captured with words the true essence and the sheer bloody hell of love. And I do love him. Oh God, oh God.

EIGHT

Sascha and Si:
Inner-City Sophisticates

Other names: apart from Yuppie (see 'What's what',
p.16–17), another acronym which had a short following
was DINK (Double Income No Kids). A possibly even
more accurate description of the lifestyle and aspirations
of the Inner-City Sophisticate is provided by the word
DINS — Double Income No Sex.

ADVANTAGES:

A comfortable and exciting lifestyle in many ways.

DISADVANTAGES:

May not sit comfortably if you have an ethical streak.
Also extremely stressful. Your job takes a lot of energy;
the constant fear that you will lose it takes even more —
the whole thing would collapse immediately if you were
retrenched (downsized).

* * * * *

This is the class most written about in the glossy magazines, which is interesting considering that it is the
smallest in terms of numbers. Whenever the magazines

publish their lists of 'What's In and What's Out', they really mean what's currently in or out for this group. When they classify people into different social groups they are talking about the subgroups of this class. And in fact there possibly are more subdivisions of this class than of others, partly because everyone is wishing to be seen as different and original, partly because one's job is such an important element of one's life in this class that the different professions tend to cluster together and form their own mini-cultures.

Some Inner-City Sophisticates are older Upper Middles whose children have left home and who are tired of keeping up the big house and garden. They use the sale of the house, which some young pregnant couple are breaking their necks to get at, to fund a new inner-city retirement. After years of cooking for the family and looking after the pool, the older and now carefree couple love eating every night at restaurants and travelling whenever they feel like it.

However, the more typical Inner-City Sophisticate is young and without children.

The look

Clothes are obviously important but it's your body language and the expression on your face that has to be mastered first.

You have to perform a double act. On the one hand it is necessary to be vibrant and amusing; but you must know how to look deadpan. You are cool, streetwise. Nothing surprises you. You must never look gloomy (boring) or upset (uncool) although cold anger against

Si and Sascha dress down for a casual breakfast.

somebody like an employee who has been an idiot is all right. Innocent enthusiasm or compassion for others is totally out.

You may need to practise in front of a mirror to perfect the art of looking utterly bored to those who don't interest you, and interesting and alive to those who do.

Sascha

'Chic' is the operative word. You are the smartest of the smart, the best-dressed of all the classes. Black is *the* inner-city colour, and it's amazing how inventive you can be with it — there's absolutely no need to look like an Italian widow. There's dull black, shiny black, black wool, black lace, black crepe. If you add white the permutations are endless. Sascha has nothing in her wardrobe except black and white and some neutrals. She has black and white spots, stripes, checks and solid blocks of colour. Large spots, small spots. Square checks, diagonal checks.

Every year there is one colour that is fashionable and one colour only. Hot pink, lime green or whatever. Every now and then the magazines make a statement such as 'white is the new black'. Much as she likes to follow trends, Sascha has the nerve to ignore the new shades and stick with black because it's her colour. Let other people follow *her* lead.

Sascha's wardrobe is based on suits and jackets, although they are very different to Caroline's. Sascha's are shorter, smaller, smarter. A short dress with a cropped jacket is perfect for the office and on to dinner. She wears linen often because it's so hard to look after. She has dresses, suits, pants, all sharply cut and all new. A few timeless plain black pieces can carry on for a couple of seasons, but the thought of wearing a jacket in the wrong shape is horrifying to Sascha. It's all very well to be an original, but not to that extent.

She likes Australian designers, but is more interested in the right look than the right label. Let Nikki show off by buying expensive brands. Sascha has higher things on her mind, such as wearing what suits her.

She owns one pair of designer track pants for walking into the gym, but does not wear them to watch television. She owns no dressing gown, petticoat nor comfortable jumper, but if she did she would call it a 'sweater'. While she is rarely out in the elements and doesn't need such a thing as an anorak, she has one camel-hair coat for overseas trips.

The right accessories, it hardly needs to be said, are crucial. Sascha owns dozens of pairs of shoes, belts and bags. Her sunglasses are totally plain and look like the sort given away in hamburger joints, although they happen to be extremely expensive. She spends a lot of time buying her jewellery. Some of this is expensive costume jewellery but what she likes most is large and striking pieces in silver which look good against black. She often wears a huge plain silver ring and a heavy silver chain with a ball. Her ideal is one stunning piece that makes a statement about her taste rather than her bank balance.

Everything is always in perfect condition — the crispness of Sascha's white shirts would almost put Dot's to shame except it's easier for Sascha because every-thing goes to the drycleaners or laundry. Stockings are as smooth as silk, shoes unscuffed.

Sascha prefers her hair to be like her coffee — black and simple. It is trimmed every week to keep the sharpness of the shape — dead straight with a fringe. Like her clothes it is always in perfect condition. If it has a natural wave she has it straightened.

Her make-up has echoes of Mary Quant and the sixties, except for the lipstick. Her skin is smooth, pale and matte. Lips are bright and eyes are dark. Extraneous facial hair and skin blemishes are not allowed. Her nails are always perfect because she doesn't have to do any housework.

Si (short for Simon)

Lives by the same rules as Sascha. Everything must be absolutely up to the minute, big city cool. If it is worn on Wall Street it's OK. Like Sascha, he strives to achieve an original image, but within prescribed limits. Eccentricity is not admired; Inner-City Sophisticates prefer to leave that to the Intellectuals. His clothes are elegant, but have some little touch that demonstrates his individuality. He wouldn't wear monogrammed shirts, but may have a metal tip to his shirt collar.

Si almost always wears a suit, but believes he has little in common with the conservative pin-striped suits from the old school. He doesn't look to the Melbourne Club or to England but towards the States or Asia; somewhere where it's happening today.

As well as looking after his fitness, Si is prepared to do whatever else it takes to look good. He has facials and manicures as a matter of course, and spends a considerable amount of money on moisturiser and body scrubs.

He may wear a ponytail, but it will be very different to Wolfgang's scruffy version. Si's is based on a good cut and is more tamed. He wears one gold earring. One of the worries of Si's life is how to be noticed without looking like a drug baron. As he always carries his mobile in his hand this is difficult.

Career

Inner-City Sophisticates can be roughly divided into two main groups — the arty and the commercial. It's not surprising that there is a lot of rivalry and contempt for the values of others, because many of the jobs are themselves a blend of the creative and the mercantile. Those who work in fields such as fashion, design, photography or advertising must be capable of original thought but also have to go through the vulgar process of finding a buyer for their work and therefore catering for the buyer's taste. This often leads them to despise themselves as much as anybody else.

Other possible areas are the media, especially journalism and especially magazine journalism. Many actors also live an Inner-City lifestyle, especially the ones who work in TV. The litmus test is whether you are likely to be mentioned in the media yourself on a regular basis. This isn't to say there aren't plenty of people working as computer salesmen or personal assistants who rent an apartment in the city, buy a mobile phone and eat out a lot. (The wannabes.)

Si works at the art gallery, which means he gets to meet *everybody* — arty Intellectuals, rich buyers, serious Upper Middles taking in their weekly diet of culture. Sascha is on a glossy lifestyle magazine. Both are somewhat vague about what it is they do, compared to who they do it for.

The house

Outside

Inner-City Sophisticates live in smart new apartments, converted warehouses and terrace houses. Cities that don't have enough old terraces to convert are busily building new ones and painting them in dull colours to look old as quickly as possible.

Inside

Sascha and Si live on the top floor of an old clothes warehouse. It's light and bright and so very New York. Their interior design is not only based on the latest in the glossy magazines but has been featured in several. (They were good moments.)

The key word is 'tasteful'. Everything in the Sophisticated apartment must go perfectly. There is no place in the decorating scheme for anything superfluous to the current look. Si and Sascha have similar tastes — it's what brought them together in the first place. However, Si is still trying to wean Sascha off her penchant for masses of cushions on the sofa and the heavy wooden bedhead she loves, which has led to some major rows. It is becoming a serious problem and they are considering counselling.

Gifts from other people are even more of a problem. (Sascha's cousin Caroline always says 'pressies', which Sascha finds very irritating.) Obviously their real friends know what they like and can be relied on to find gorgeous pieces on their overseas trips. They would never embarrass Si and Sascha by buying some hideous thing that spoils the entire look of the apartment, but their families are another matter altogether. Practically everything Si's mother gives them has to be discarded. Luckily she doesn't visit often — living so far away — so they can keep her gifts in the spare room and bring them

out when she arrives. However, this is a first class
nuisance and Si is realising that he will have to find some
way of subtly letting her know that her taste is appalling.
If she could only appreciate the natural, sincere style
they have strived so hard to achieve in the place.

They were furious that black and white went out
just when they had eliminated all colour from their
decorating scheme. For some time they have had a
purple velvet couch with red cushions, but now that
neutrals are coming back they will probably have to
start again. Si is excited about this because he feels that
the artwork he brings home will look even better
against a pale background. Both Si and Sascha predict
that suede and light-coloured timbers will become
even more popular. Neither can ever see the mini-
malist look going out of fashion. There are many
photos around the apartment, all enlarged, grainy,
black-and-white prints.

It's just a pity that having made the place so perfect, they actually spend most of their time elsewhere.

The lifestyle

Food

Food is important and, like everything else, must be new
and different. Si and Sascha are both dedicated foodies
and read cookery books and magazines avidly. The
kitchen is crammed with appliances — one of Sascha's
favourite weekend pastimes is browsing the gourmet
homeware shops. She and Si give each other little fun
presents all the time — an olive spoon, a strawberry

huller, bird's beak scissors. They have a collection of knives that would do a butcher proud.

They only ever buy the freshest of fresh ingredients, which tends to mean Australian rather than imported. Australian salmon, baby emu, milk-fed lamb. If it's hard to get hold of and Dot and Brian or, better still, Caroline and Richard haven't heard of it then Si and Sascha feel they must be onto a good thing. They're considering buying a glass-door fridge so that everyone can see they don't fill it with TV dinners or cheap wine. They don't have a garden as such, but do grow fresh herbs in pots.

The right bread is important. Si and Sascha can spot a fake wannabe a mile off anyway, but the bread they order in a restaurant confirms it. Anyone who wants old-fashioned white bread with — Si can hardly believe it — butter, is so suburban it's embarrassing. Most Inner-City Sophisticates can't remember who invented the bread test, although it began about the time of bagels. Other people don't have their subtle sensitivity and taste and can't quite see how these differ from an ordinary salad roll, giving themselves away immediately.

Water is another thing that must be got right. They have the purifier in the kitchen, and Sascha carries bottled water with her at all times. However, now that teenagers from the outer suburbs are also carrying bottles of water to school, she's unsure whether this is still a good idea.

Wine

Si knows a lot about wine and is happy to share his knowledge with others. He has been going to courses for a couple of years now, but has enough sense to keep quiet about them. He knows what's what, and isn't about to betray his origins by displaying ignorance of anything. Sascha likes everyone to think their background included a decanter of port passed around the table at Christmas, rather than the one bottle of sparkling wine which had to last for the whole day.

A SIMPLE LIFE

Neither Si nor Sascha believe that the grotty details of life should be allowed to interfere with living so they pay other people to do all the boring chores. They feel good about this — it provides work for so many people. Someone comes in to clean and iron. Most of their clothes go to the drycleaners or the laundry. Sascha has a personal shopper who knows her size, colours and taste. They don't use the car every day but it's handy for weekends away, so someone has to look after that.

Si is proud that he doesn't own any tools — not so much as a screwdriver. Sally has no sewing machine.

Although they are both, of course, marvellous cooks, they don't get to do it as often as they would like. Lunch is always eaten out, naturally, since they both work. Breakfast is usually eaten at their favourite café because they so often have breakfast meetings that it's just easier to get into the habit, and dinner is often out at a party, restaurant or friend's home.

The week

Life is busy, busy, busy. Work, parties, openings, lunches, launches. They are seen everywhere, and feel proud to be on so many mailing lists. It's expensive, of course, buying all those tickets, but hey, they can afford it and they both get an enormous buzz out of mixing with so many well-known faces. Obviously they wouldn't dream of asking anyone for an autograph, although Si's mother boasts to everyone she meets that her son knows her favourite soapie stars. Both Si and Sascha have a dream that one day someone will pay *them* to attend an opening.

There isn't a day goes by but Sascha doesn't give thanks that she was lucky enough to meet Si. She loved being a single girl about town of course, and she still keeps in touch with the girls she used to flat-share with, but there were so many girls and so few men who weren't married or gay. Singles bars were just too awful, and she was *determined* that she wouldn't go back to the suburbs like her friend Clare, who was just on the verge of making it big-time, but ended up throwing it all away to marry a boy she had known at school.

Sunday brunch

One of their favourite ways of relaxing is having Sunday brunch with their very good friends Leon and Rupert at their absolutely *gorgeous* terrace house. Although Leon owns an antique shop, he has been marvellously restrained in decorating the house, with just one or two beautiful pieces in each room.

They eat in the back courtyard, which is Mediterranean at its most perfect. The fountain, the terracotta pots, the vine covering the high brick wall, the olive trees, window shutters, the iron and wood chairs. The food is superb — that's Rupert's department — the wine the best.

After a stressful week, they find it a relief to sit back and relax. The company couldn't be bettered — everybody is both witty and beautiful — and ready to indulge in delicious gossip. Between them all they seem to know everybody who's anybody. Leon is in top form and being very funny. The usual jokes about how boring it is that Si and Sascha are straight. Sascha sometimes gets tired of some of the innuendoes about Si's sexuality. If anybody should know, surely it's her!

After lunch an invigorating discussion about the row at the art gallery. Everyone getting involved and taking sides. Sascha very proud of Si who, knowing the story from the inside, was able to hold the floor for some time. Won't do his career any harm at all, considering the number of important people present.

* * * * *

Si and Sascha have every intention of going on and living their present lifestyle forever, even after children arrive. They are such organised people they can't see what the problem will be. Everything is ready, the baby will soon fit into their routine, and their children will benefit from a cosmopolitan upbringing. The park is nearby — who needs a garden?

Eighteen months after their first child is born Sascha, who is already an exhausted crying wreck, finds herself pregnant again. They give up and run for cover in the suburbs, exchanging their lovely apartment for a traditional house and large garden. However, they are positive this is only a temporary hitch.

TYPICAL SASCHA E-MAIL

From: lifestyle@city.com.au
Sent: Tuesday 2 March
To: Penelope
Subject: personal

Pen, Have you heard about Clare? I could hardly believe it. Have you seen him? We had them over for lunch last week. Wanted to go out but couldn't think of anywhere suitable where we wouldn't know anyone. Suppose we'll have to go to the wedding, although Si says he'll make sure he's out of the country that weekend. Don't blame him, although I said Thank You Very Much. Am I supposed to go on my own?

Work frantic as usual. Hardly time to do anything, but always marvellous to hear from you. Lunch soon?

Ciao
Sascha

NINE

Sally and John: Country Folk

Other names: squatters, cockies, country cousins,
country bumpkins, hicks, hillbillies

ADVANTAGES:

Extremely satisfying lifestyle when all goes well.

DISADVANTAGES:

A disaster if it goes wrong.

* * * * *

Tucked away in a corner of many people's minds is a yearning to find the perfect spot in the country, to get away from it all, to live a peaceful life. There is a distinct possibility that it could be quite different — snakes and flies, drought and floods, isolation — but that won't stop people from giving it a go. I would suggest though that if you don't like horses you should definitely think again.

Sally and John reckon up the spoils of the day.

The look

John

There are several distinct Country looks, especially for men. On the one hand there is the famous moleskins, pale blue shirt and Akubra look — the closest thing we have to an internationally recognised uniform, even though so few wear it. On the other hand there is the hillbilly look of tight dark jeans, checked shirt with large, old-fashioned hat and a suggestion of straw hanging from the mouth. For everyday wear John often goes for a middle-of-the-road, go-anywhere style. Good quality blue jeans, a mid-blue shirt, cap when he's working.

But, having inherited his farm, he also feels comfortable in the squatter look, and certainly on sale day he wouldn't dress any other way. The moleskins, cotton sheep-cocky shirt (epaulettes, two pockets), and his Cooper's Sheepdip diary in his pocket. He also wears his flat, low-crowned Akubra hat and R.M. Williams elastic-sided boots. These are tan and flat-soled, very different to the black, high-heeled, cowboy boots worn in outback cattle country. With the boots, the stockmen would wear blue jeans and checked shirts, or worse, shiny bright shirts with the round shape of a tobacco tin showing through at the pocket.

Other possibilities for boots are Blundstones (Blunnies) or Rossies. Blunnies are cheaper. A pocket knife in a leather pouch on the belt is OK — just. If you live in a wet, cold area a Drizabone is fine for when you are actually outside rescuing a sheep from a bog. However, it looks silly worn to town on a hot day or in the pub on Saturday night.

When you go to the city you can wear your drill pants, tweedy jacket and Akubra. Add a pale blue shirt and a wool tie. While this look brands you distinctly as country and will attract a certain amount of amused looks, it's probably safer than trying to keep up with city styles when you don't live there all the time. However hard you try, you will always look comically out of date. There are various Country outfitters, but for newcomers an R.M. Williams shop is a good starting point.

The other indicator of the Countryman is the lined red face. It's strange that while this is a result of long hours in the hot sun, it never looks remotely like the tan you get from lying on the beach. Likewise John's sun-bleached, straw-like hair doesn't in any way resemble the surfie's pale locks.

Sally

The more aristocratic the woman, the more likely she is to spend much of her time in moleskin pants, a pale shirt and riding boots. The average woman, however, especially if she doesn't ride, is better to wear a modified version of the Upper Middle look. Sally buys a range of skirts, slacks and pants, shirts, a couple of jackets, a plain leather belt, a beret and a raffia hat. Jumpers are plain wool and worn with a white shirt collar showing. Some type of warm quilted jacket is essential — doling out soup from the boot of the car at a horsey event on a cold winter's day you could almost think you were at an English point to point. This ward-robe will take you anywhere in the day. For evening a plain white silky shirt and long black skirt or evening pants is all that's needed.

Sally's hair will be short or medium length, depending on how windy and dusty her surroundings are. Unlike Nikki, Sally can wear an Alice band without looking ridiculous. Her skin has a healthy scrubbed look — a nice, open-air, reliable-looking face is considered very attractive.

Sally has expensive but unobtrusive jewellery, not unlike Caroline's. John wears none, not even a wedding ring, because he might catch it on machinery or in a gate and tear off a finger.

GOING BUSH

You have to consider whether you want to be a weekend country squire or do the thing properly and live in the bush full-time. Many people feel they can have the best of both worlds by living and working in the city during the week and heading off to the country on Friday night, but that rarely works out well. Apart from the sheer nuisance of always packing and unpacking, if you try this you will find you never fully belong in either world. You can't take part in weekend activities with your city friends and you will be despised by the locals in the country.

Better to take the plunge, move there permanently and make every effort to become integrated, although ten years is usually the minimum before you will be considered a local.

Where?

Find a couple of hectares (but call them acres) a few kilometres (miles) from a medium-sized town, which is itself a few hours by road and/or train from the city. It's all very well to have romantic dreams, but can you really do without your morning paper and a cappuccino now and then?

Unlike real Country people, who are anchored to one spot by the farm (probably unsaleable) and family ties, you can go where you like.

Jobs for the boys

You will probably find that the only sensible option is to buy a small property and earn your living some other

way than off the land, given that few people have the
necessary millions needed to buy a working farm. In
conversation, however, you will have to treat your paying
job as unimportant and the property as the mainstay of
your existence. This is especially important if your job is
essentially city-based — public servant in the nearest
town, for instance. Some jobs are OK in their own right —
if John was a stock and station agent or a farm vet, he
could wear moleskins, his Drizabone and an Akubra at
any time of the day or night without looking like a pretentious dickhead.

Ideally, you have enough money (we're talking
millions again) to get into something like grapes. It
means you're growing things, as farmers do, but grapes
mean wine, which is more of a city thing — the best of
both worlds. Unusual animals like alpacas are another
bet. It's not absolutely clear what the point of raising
some of these animals is, except to sell them at high
prices to other new farmers.

You could also start a boutique bed-and-breakfast
business. You will need to search the second-hand shops
for brass bedsteads, floral china jug and basin sets, and
interesting old chairs and pictures — if they're not your
ancestors, who's to know? It's also a decided advantage if
either Sally or John is a gourmet cook.

Sally

It's easier for single women. A woman can marry a farmer and have done with it — Sally became a bona fide
Countrywoman the minute the wedding ring went on
her finger. The traditional method for women to achieve

this was to go as a teacher or a nurse to a country town. In the fifties and sixties the local farmers would line up to meet the train bringing the new teachers to town, ready to take their pick.

While this has gone, it is still easy enough for a woman to marry a farmer, should she so wish. Given the exodus of young people from the bush, Sally, with bankable teaching skills, was snapped up fast. The serious drawback is that she then has to share every aspect of her life, including her bank account, with her husband's family.

As for the squatters' sons, the situation is the same as it ever was and ever will be. If you're not one of them, don't bother to apply. His wife will have been picked out for him long ago.

Very, very occasionally, once in a blue moon, a man may find a farmer's daughter looking for a husband to work the farm and eventually inherit it. If this happens, good luck to you, although you may find you have to serve a long and difficult apprenticeship as the idiot son-in-law who can do nothing right.

The house

Outside

There is almost as great a variety of housing in the country as the city except that, when building new houses, Country people have, on the whole, had the sense to steer clear of the Tuscan look, recognising its basic incompatibility with our climate.

John's brother having inherited the family home, he and Sally have built one of the newer classic homestead styles. It's on the side of a hill, single storey, long and low, with an iron roof, verandahs on all sides with wooden pillars and a bull-nosed roof. French windows open onto the front verandah from the main bedroom, lounge room and dining room. The whole thing is surrounded by sloping lawns, flowering shrubs, lots of rose bushes, woodchip paths, a few exotic trees and several large gums a safe distance from the house (bushfires.)

The front verandah is used occasionally, when Sally and John have guests. The back verandah gets most use and has a homely, comfortable look. To achieve it, you need a few old chairs or benches, hooks for the many coats, jackets and hats, boots of various shapes and sizes, a dead car battery, wooden crates of vegetables and a couple of rabbit traps. Once there would have been a rifle or two, but that would be asking for trouble today.

Inside

Long gone are the days of roughing it in the bush. There's no reason why the inside of your house can't look very like the Middle Australian or Upper Middle house, depending on how much cash and time you have available.

In John and Sally's house the living areas are open plan, like the modern Middle Australian city house, although nobody has ever been known to enter it from the front door except, now and then, a religious caller. There are two other entrances: one at the laundry door, so the men can leave their boots outside on the back verandah and wash their hands on the way in for lunch, and one at the end of the verandah.

The long hallway and the family and kitchen areas need a hard-wearing and dirt-hiding floor, like slate or cork. The lounge and dining rooms are well furnished, with soft carpet, thick drapes, comfortable couches and chairs, occasional tables with many vases of flowers (the big garden) and a large and efficient wood-burning fire. Walls are covered in photos of dogs, horses and prize-winning stock.

As in most family houses the kitchen/meals/family area is used most, and needs a large serving bench as the centrepiece. Not only is Sally kept busy cooking meals for a lot of people on regular occasions, but John has to have somewhere to put all the paperwork — accounts, manuals, instructions for sheep dip — plus the tractor pieces and samples of this and that. In the summer the fire radio crackles day and night, along with the two-way. Sally gets sick of it one day and turns it off, to John's extreme annoyance, because that is the day he runs out of fuel and has to walk all the way home from the far paddock.

Squattocracy

If you have the cash you can do the traditional Country house look — in many ways the most sought after of all looks and lifestyles. John's brother James lives in a big square house with a slate roof, white wooden turned verandah posts and shutters on the French windows, a wide central hallway with large rooms opening off it, furnished in something heavy like mahogany. Walls are pale, and floors a mix of polished boards with dark rugs, fitted carpets, and sisal matting.

Furnishings and decorations are similar to the city Upper Middle house, except that everything is on a bigger scale, and possibly older. Many of these houses have billiard rooms, huge sweeps of heavy curtains, iron bedsteads, colonial furniture, American quilts on beds, flowers everywhere, silver, old-fashioned prints. There will be open fires in every room — all that free wood — and a wood-burning range in the kitchen. (The famous English Aga is the prototype.) Grandmother's house in *My Brilliant Career* said it exactly.

The drawback is that, as in *My Brilliant Career*, you also need an army of servants to run it.

JOINING IN

John

To be fully integrated into the community you need to adopt that dry, laconic wit that involves sending up yourself as well as everybody around you. It is based on a pragmatic fatalistic acceptance that, in the end, it's all a waste of time. The weather will get you, the crops will fail, stock will die, the government will change the rules. It is supposed to be typically Australian humour, but has all but died out in the cities where people take themselves so bloody seriously these days

For John, all this is straightforward enough. He wears his oldest jeans, a clean shirt and the elastic-sided boots and drives the battered Holden ute to the pub. Everybody knows him and his entire family history, so all he has to do is not be too stuck up to drink in the public bar and the locals love him. The newcomer has to put in a bit more effort. Lean on the bar, look weary but relaxed, be prepared to buy a beer for anyone near you, and agree with every criticism of the government, the merits of the local football club, the idiocy of city people. Mention on every possible occasion how glad you are to be free of the rat race.

The new boy will also have to show that he's no mug. Everybody in the district will be waiting for him to make some slip-up — they love stories of city slickers who thought the bull was a cow. He has to listen to the advice of old hands, but show he's got a few clues of his own. Mostly, he has to get his hands dirty. He will have to go to every working bee that's on and work harder than anybody else, attend every fire and if possible do something heroic that shows he's a real man.

Sally

Sally had to make more of an effort, but eventually worked her way in through the school. If you don't have children then adopt some fast, because Country people always have children. The new Countrywoman will have to attend every assembly, every open day and P&C meeting, and probably volunteer for a committee. She will also bake cakes and jams to sell at fund-raising stalls. (Hint: If you're a hopeless cook you can buy the more expensive chunky jams and chutneys in the city, and soak off the labels.)

To be really accepted, Sally has to shop locally, despite the high prices, because it is considered a betrayal not to support local businesses. However, nobody has to know if you stock the pantry on your city trips, provided you spend some time every day in the local store, and stop to talk to everyone you meet.

There are many clubs and societies Sally can join. While the CWA (that is, the Country Women's Association) is starting to lose members — all those bossy women with hairy chins and thick legs — it is being rapidly replaced by arty things like book clubs and drama associations.

HORSES

There are two breeds of horsey people — the little bandy-legged jockey types who live near the city, and the tall, elegant, polo-playing types. You naturally want to be one of the latter, although it isn't necessary to actually play polo, which is a fearsomely expensive sport. Instead, you can either do the pony club circuit with the children or play polocrosse, which is something of a poor relation to polo (being partly based on netball it could hardly be anything else) but has the major advantage of needing only one horse per player.

There should be bridles, hard hats and riding boots left all over verandahs and laundries. A horse blanket with a bright embroidered name is another special touch. Sally's horses are considered to be almost family members.

* * * * *

You need to be very sure beforehand that this is the class you want to join, because once you've thrown in your job, sold your city house and gone bush it can be very humiliating and embarrassing, not to say wildly expensive, to go back with your tail between your legs, because you found that you hated being away from the city.

City people are often irritated and amused by John and Sally appearing to put on superior airs and graces. It has to be said that sometimes they do, but only, of course, as consolation to themselves for the inconveniences and isolation they have to put up with.

SALLY TO HER FRIEND LIZ

'Blue Vistas'
Sunday 4th

Dear Liz

Glad you're enjoying Europe so much. Sometimes wish I was still young and fancy free. Can't see us getting away for ages, there's always some drama happening on the property. Not that this seems to stop James and Sarah from getting away for plenty of weekends! You know how I feel about John's brother and the whole set-up here. John does everything and they do nothing, but they complain every time we need anything, like the new car. The station wagon was literally falling to pieces under us, but you should have heard the carry-on when we bought the 4WD. Of course they had to go out and buy one just like ours. So childish.

Enough complaining. Although I must admit there are times when I could kill to get my hands on that house.

The annual show was the big event here recently. Would you believe I won first prize for my bottled fruit? My mother-in-law was very proud of me! (And Sarah's nose was out of joint, believe me.) Sometimes feel like shocking the natives by turning up in black leather, but of course played it safe and wore the usual brushed cotton skirt, classic white shirt, plain jacket and flat shoes. Must say though, that John looked good in his tweeds.

Do you remember Rhonda, who was working for me last time you were here? Ran into her in the tea tent and she asked after you. I ignored the tattoos and pierced nose. After all, when you think of her family!!

Did the usual thing of all meeting under the big tree for lunch. The women compete like mad to produce the best food, which is tedious, because you know how I loathe cooking. I insisted on us all going to the pub for tea.

The children are doing well at school. I do miss them during term time, and long for the holidays. We went down last weekend and saw them all. Julie had the lead role in 'Guys and Dolls' and Andrew was captaining the rugby side. We also caught up with a few friends and went to see Les Mis. Are you planning to see it in London?

Times are tough here, but we manage. Looking forward to seeing you here for Christmas as usual, unless you've met some fascinating English lord by then!

With love
Sally

TEN

Barb and Bob: Middle Australians

If you haven't recognised yourself in this book it's probably because you're one of the vast number of people who consider themselves to be in the middle (you like to describe yourself as classless).

The great attraction of this class is that you live a comfortable lifestyle without having to worry about a whole lot of snobberies and conventions. You won't have to cook foods you've never heard of, learn all about classical music, or make up interesting lies about your past. On the other hand you don't have to be obsessive about having a clean and trim house. There are rules but they're more a case of don't do this or that (pick your nose in public and so on) rather than prescribing what you must do.

There is a lot of movement into and out of this class. It is the aim, the goal, the dream of many poor or Lower Middles to be considered Middle Class. It is the aim of many Middles to be considered Upper Middles or Intellectuals. Younger Middles may see themselves more as Inner-City Sophisticates.

Barb prepares to spend the next month congratulating Bob on his culinary efforts today.

The look

Clothes are less important to Middle Australians than to almost any other group. The house, car, the children's schooling are what matter.

Barb

Given the sheer size of the Middle Class, there is a wide variation in style, sophistication and cost of clothes. On a good day Barb can look as classically elegant as Caroline. On a bad day she looks as sloppy as Sharon's mother, Mavis. Most of the time she looks not unlike Dot, only bigger.

Barb wears dresses, slacks and skirts. She shops at all the big department stores and the women's clothing chains. She has a lot of clothes in no particular style or colour, buying things she likes at the time. She is always clean and tidy, but not as finicky as Dot — she'll wear something a couple of times before washing it. She admires Caroline's taste, but can't bring herself to spend hundreds of dollars on a handbag when she knows that Peter needs a new tennis racquet.

Hair could be any colour but will always be in a neat bob of some sort, becoming shorter as Barb gets older. This class believes most strongly in the adage that a woman over forty shouldn't wear long hair. Make-up will come from the mid-price department store ranges. If nothing else, Barb always wears lipstick.

Barb has quite a collection of jewellery. Much of it came from the family in one way or another — either presents from the children, or passed down from aunts and grandmothers. She has both silver and gold, pearls and marquisite. She rarely buys jewellery for herself, but when she does it is either good-quality costume jewellery or moderately priced silver or gold pieces.

Bob

Bob isn't too fussed about clothes either, but he likes to look respectable and reasonably prosperous. He wears clothes similar to Richard's, although in a cheaper version. He couldn't care less about labels. He doesn't believe that real men like clothes or clothes shopping, and is more than happy for Barb to buy all his clothes.

He is used to wearing a shirt and tie to work and looks comfortable in a suit, but is most happy in jeans and a soft shirt. Working on the car at the weekend he wears black shorts and a T-shirt, but changes out of them before going anywhere. On a beach or fishing holiday he spends his whole time in an old pair of baggy shorts and a variety of polo shirts.

Bob's hair is fairly short and cut in a standard, somewhat nondescript style every couple of weeks. He never wears cosmetics of any sort, nor jewellery other than a wedding ring.

The house

The house is the most important indicator of Middle Australian status, as well as a focus of the Middle Australian family's time and money. They're lucky. Because their house is so much bigger and better to start with, Barb and Bob can afford to be less fussy than Dot and Brian, but still achieve more satisfying results.

Given their sheer force of numbers, Middle Australian homes are found just about everywhere, except in the very richest and poorest suburbs. Middle Australian houses are found in country towns and on farms. They tend, however, to be thickest in that middle belt of suburbs between the Inner-City Sophisticates and Intellectuals — Middles like a bit of green around them — and the outer metropolitan areas of really cheap housing.

The large number of Middle Australian houses can be roughly divided into two types: old and new.

The older house

Outside

Old doesn't mean old as in Upper Middle Federation or inner-city poor and falling down, but old as in substantial forties or fifties house. It will probably be solid brick and vaguely Californian bungalow, although it may well be rendered and vaguely Spanish. It will look *almost* as neat as the Lower Middle house, but everything will be on a much larger scale. For instance, the lawn won't be a small strip on either side of a path, but will cover the whole front yard, with a driveway down the side.

You can do a lot to establish yourself as Middle Australian by becoming a complete bore about roses and telling everybody else what they have done wrong in pruning their bushes.

Inside

The interior of the older Middle Australian house tends to be somewhat dark — dark carpet, dark wooden picture rail, fairly heavy furniture. The curtains (window treatments) will be heavy and lined — possibly velvet. The fireplace surrounds will be dark. The rooms are quite large but the windows and doors are small, letting in little light to brighten everything up. As well, there are pictures and ornaments covering every possible space. Many of the photos are studio photos of the whole family dressed in their best. They are black and white but hand-tinted in pinkish shades. They never look quite like their subjects and visitors have trouble recognising them.

The typical house has a substantial square hallway with dark polished boards and a rug, or a fitted carpet of dark red floral swirls. Leadlight doors lead into the lounge and dining rooms. Against one wall a half oval table holds an old-fashioned-looking cream and gold telephone sitting on a white doily, with a cut glass vase next to it containing real roses from the garden. An old-fashioned light fitting — cream glass — hangs from the centre of the hallway.

Barb's lounge room is comfortable with a variety of chairs and couches. They will tend to be very full and rounded, well-sprung, with some sort of feature made of the arms; they may be wooden. Next to the fireplace, which works, there is a brass firewood basket and a set of brass tongs and poker. On the mantelpiece are more vases and some expensive china ornaments such as Lladro figurines. The glass-fronted china cabinet holds Barb's quite impressive collection of china. A full set of a well-known brand, some cup, saucer and plate sets — of different shapes, sizes and patterns — and the silver tea service she was given when she left work to get married.

The older Middle Australian house always has an old-fashioned sideboard — probably of thirties vintage — with the bottles on top. Whisky, gin, port, sherry, an exotic liqueur or two. On top will also be a couple of family photos, although most of them are in the photo albums in the bookcase. If Barb is into collecting spoons or thimbles or whatever, they go here as well.

Bookshelves hold mostly books (as opposed to pictures or ornaments) — novels and reference books, Barb and Bob's old school textbooks. There will be a couple of whimsical older books — often the old School Readers — a lot of National Geographics and a few quality magazines.

Barb and Bob have a queen-size bed, with a matching set of headboards, bedside tables, and dressing table. The set is in one of the darker woods and looks as though it's been in the house since it was built, which can't be the case since queen-size beds hadn't been invented then. The bed would once have had an eiderdown but Barb and Bob have discovered the convenience of doonas, although they sometimes put them on top of blankets and sheets, which defeats the purpose of their design.

The secondary bedrooms are quite large, but there aren't many of them, because in the days when the house was built children had to share rooms. To overcome this, Bob enclosed the side and back verandahs. Even so, the children's rooms are still extremely cluttered, full of books, projects of various kinds, their own and their parents' old toys, and sporting equipment.

The kitchen is always of a later style than the rest of the house — late seventies but with any luck minus the orange. It is a large room, although not entirely convenient to work in. The veneer cupboards with some sort of detail etched in catch the dust very nicely. The original wood stove is still there, although not used. Barb sits the microwave on top of the hotplate. The dining room is mostly used for formal occasions as Barb and Bob usually eat at the table in the sunroom.

Inside, the older Middle Australian house is not dissimilar to the Upper Middle house.

The new house

There are also vast numbers of Middle Australians buying up new houses in the many housing estates being built on the edges of all our cities — the ones where they leave some trees behind — not those hideous tracts of nothingness where they demolish everything in sight and put up five hundred identical boxes.

The new house will usually be of brick, unless you want to make an environmental statement by having some new material with efficient insulating properties. You're not as environmentally conscious as the Upper Middles or Intellectuals, but you do like value for money and anything that saves on power bills can only be good.

The house will be quite large, and generally of an irregular shape. It could be of almost any style under the sun, from Tudor to Tuscan. Whatever the period represented, it will manage to have a vaguely American look, rather than English. There should be soaring rooflines, gables, double garages, fences and low walls going here and there. If nobody can find the front door many Middle Australians feel they've got it right.

Inside

The key words are 'new' and 'modern'. The basic look is open plan — a big, irregular hallway with rooms leading off all over the place, with very few doors. The hallway floor will be covered in very hard shiny tiles. The walls may be white, pale cream or a pastel colour.

The master bedroom is at the front, with an enormous ensuite bathroom attached. The bedroom itself will be large, with a queen- or king-size bed. Barb covers it in an expensive bedspread, not dissimilar to Dot's, but in a heavy brocade rather than nylon. The living room and dining room flow easily into one another. The carpet is thick and pale, the furniture fairly heavy-looking, even if veneer. Mock rosewood is a popular choice. Everything — dining table and chairs, coffee table, sideboard, wall unit, bookshelves — is in the same style. To be absolutely certain of this, Barb buys them all at the same time.

A very large wall unit covers one entire wall. Barb's best china and cut glass bowls are in here, and one section has books. At all times Barb has something on the dining-room table — candelabra, a vase of dried flowers. On the odd occasion when the dining table is used, she puts real flowers in the vase. Barb tries so hard with the house but has periodic battles with Bob over furnishings. She managed to stop him buying the coffee table made from a single, heavy, irregular cross-section of timber, but he insisted on the clock in the shape of Australia. Barb makes a point of telling everyone that Bob chose it.

The most important part of the house is the kitchen/family/games area. The kitchen is large and has very modern fittings — an enormous fridge/freezer, dishwasher, central workspace and so on. The serving bench will open onto the family room and be covered by papers — school notices, newspapers, bills, etc.

House designs change regularly and builders are creative about naming rooms. If a display home has an upmarket name there will be a library and a music room. Others feature home theatres, computer rooms, galleries, banquet rooms, studios, a winter room and a summer room, activity rooms, retreats.

Despite these different names, the most fascinating thing about modern Middle Australian houses is that they are all exactly the same. People from older suburbs have to look up the street directory every time they visit, because they can never remember which friend lives in which house.

The garden

The garden of the new house will be a real feature. Depending on the climate and budget, it could be tropical, native, American colonial, English Tudor or whatever. Barb buys a good garden design book, chooses a theme and Bob follows it to the letter.

Whatever the theme, the rule is generally to keep it as plain and maintenance free as possible. No fence, a sweep of sloping lawn — the mower man cuts it — a clump of conifers, some flowering shrubs, but mostly glossy-leaved, non-flowering shrubs. The look is somewhat spoiled by the large basketball ring and backboard that is attached to the front of the garage. This isn't very attractive, but it makes a loud statement: 'We care about our kids. We want them to play sport and therefore grow up healthy and happy.'

The back of the house has a large pergola, brick paved, with an expensive table and chair setting. The barbecue is gas, and there are pot plants everywhere — especially large ferns of various kinds. Barb and Bob's pool is brick, but fibreglass is acceptable, especially if it is rectangular. Whatever the theme of the rest of the garden, there are always tropical plants near the pool.

Bob has a large shed/garage to house the cars and boat. He has a lot of power tools because they're fun to play with, but he can't always find the time to use them on the things that need mending around the house. Barb has to threaten to pay someone else to do things before Bob can get motivated.

A word about housing estates

Middles tend to appreciate those new estates surrounded by brick walls where covenants apply to stop you from working on your car in your driveway, owning a dog or doing anything that might offend anybody or reduce house prices (referred to as 'the value of the property').The Lower Middles love the concept but can't afford the prices.The Upper Middles think the whole idea is ludicrous and Middle Class. 'Typical' is the word they would use.

The Seriously Rich like the idea of being shut away from the rabble, but generally prefer to make more of an individual statement with their houses. (For instance, they love to buy six blocks and demolish the existing houses or to cause a new road to be built especially to service their three-storey mansions.)

The Intellectuals are incensed at the divisive nature of such estates and feel they can understand why the very poor write graffiti all over the walls. The Upper Class have never heard of them.

The lifestyle

The battle of the sexes

Much as she loves him, Barb often feels she is fighting a losing battle to civilise Bob, who likes to think of himself as a Real Aussie bloke who doesn't give a stuff what anybody thinks of him. He looks forward all year to the annual fishing trip with his mates. They drink an enormous amount of beer, eat rubbish food, talk dirty, fart loudly and don't wash for a week. Barb satisfies her Upper Middle fantasies by having lunch with her smart friends and joining the right clubs. As long as Bob keeps out of the way all is well.

Housework

Barb has a problem with housework. Unlike Dot, she doesn't enjoy doing it, but unlike Sharon or Virginia she can't stand having a dirty house. Unlike Caroline, Sascha, Sally and Nikki she can't afford to pay someone else to do it. Bob is useless and the kids are too busy. Barb dreams of the day when she can retire to a small easy-clean house with no kids messing it all up every five minutes.

THE CHRISTMAS LETTER

Hi everyone.

Barb and Bob catching up with you all. I always said I'd never come to this, but we just get busier every year! It has been a full year with the usual ups and downs but on the whole a good one.

Bob's business just grows and grows. He took on two more staff in March which has meant that Barb is kept busy with the books. Not that we are complaining! Bob isn't able to get away on the boat as much as he would like, but managed to catch a few fish on the annual 'Men's Weekend'. Peter went for the first time this year. A wonderful bonding experience for father and son.

Peter started well at Uni. As a scholarship winner he is put under more pressure than most to succeed, but is managing to live up to expectations. Linda is doing very well at her new job. Her boss said he had never had anyone pick it up so quickly. Wendy and Paul both had a good year at school. Paul won the History and Geography prize and Wendy the citizenship award. We don't like to boast but we are certainly proud of our kids!

Barb keeps busy looking after them all, and is considering taking up study herself this year. There's life in the old girl yet!

We had a worrying time in July when Bob's father had a few health problems, but you will be glad to hear he is now doing fine. The rest of us keep fighting fit.

Have a Happy Christmas and a wonderful year from the whole gang.

Barb, Bob, Linda, Peter, Paul, Wendy

THE AUSTRALIA DAY BARBECUE

Barb and Bob have been hosting this event for years now. All their friends, relations and acquaintances are invited. The garden looks green and beautiful, the new shade awning is set up near the pool, and Bob spends the morning cleaning the pool and getting the barbecue ready.

As well as all the cold meats, Barb and the other women marinate chicken and steak, and buy a stack of sausages for the kids. Barb makes her famous potato salad, as well as a green salad, rice salad and anything else that takes her fancy in the *Women's Weekly* cookbooks. The table is set with knives and forks, paper plates, bread and rolls. Dips and patés keep everybody going until the men have finished watching the cricket and tennis on TV and can get on with cooking the meat.

The bar fridge is working overtime although nobody gets pissed and ugly except Uncle Reg, whom everybody tactfully ignores. Given the paranoia about random breath-testing, most of the women stick to soft drink and one glass of wine so they will be able to drive home safely.

The men stand around the barbecue with their cans of beer listening to Bob talk about his new boat. Barb has to laugh at the idea of Bob cooking — most of the time he would starve if left to his own devices. The women chat and keep an eye on the kids, who are either inside playing computer games or risking their necks on the trampoline. They all admire Barb's new outdoor setting of large oval table and six comfortable chairs.

Daughter Linda's glamorous new friend from work, Sascha, has dropped in on her way to another party and is amazed to find her cousin Caroline present. How extraordinary that she can't even visit the outer suburbs without knowing someone. She tells everyone that Richard is working, but actually he threw a tantrum and said he just couldn't face a meal of burnt chops. Peter and his mates say hello to everyone, grab some food and then head off to the beach. Bob's cousin Richard is discussing his latest renovations disaster with Donny (one of Bob's apprentices). Despite Donny's tattoos, Richard is impressed by his knowledge.

Caroline, who feels a little bored, is wondering whether to ask for a paper napkin or be democratic and talk about serviettes like everybody else. Dot and Brian, who used to be Barb and Bob's neighbours when they lived in their first house, are pleased that Barb and Bob seem to have done well for themselves, but can't help noticing that there are cobwebs all over the ceiling of the pergola.

Nikki and Mike are happy to catch up with old friends now and then to remind themselves of how the other half live, but are profoundly thankful they brought their own champagne after seeing the wine that is on offer.

Everyone is sorry that John and Sally couldn't get away from the farm; John is always such witty company. However, everyone, especially Bob, is glad that Barb's sister Virginia pulled out because of a rally she had to attend. Bob doesn't mind Virginia but that bloody supercilious Wolfgang always starts an argument about something. Last time he was here he bored everybody by going on and on about Australia's iniquitous class system, and how unfair it all is. Sharon's husband Kev took what he said the wrong way and threatened to punch him and it was all very unpleasant.

As Brian said after Wolfgang had left, 'We don't *have* a class system in this country.'

ELEVEN

Whaddaya do for a crust?

Choose your occupation with care. It is one of the most obvious indicators of your class. For instance, a carpenter could become Upper Middle, but would have to work that much harder than, say, a dentist.

Real Aussies

Real Aussies are tradesmen of all kinds — the plumbers, carpenters, plasterers, bricklayers and so on. They may work for someone else or own their own business. They are also truck-drivers, storemen, barmaids and waitresses, wharfies, garbage-collectors, fishermen, cleaners or factory workers. They do any job that involves a lot of sweat and physical effort, often outside in all weathers.

Lower Middles

Lower Middles tend to have what might be termed respectable jobs, often in a service industry. They are the police, fire brigade officers, postal workers, hairdressers, taxi drivers, bus drivers, ambulance officers and shop assistants. There are many of them in the armed services, and they are also to be found in the lower ranks of the

Mike and Donny find common conversational ground.

public service. Bank tellers and clerks are typical Lower Middle jobs.

There are a few manual workers — some carpenters and factory foremen may live Lower Middle lives — although on the whole manual workers tend towards the more blokey, down-to-earth atmosphere of the Real Aussie.

Upper Middles

Anything business/professional is suitable: GPs, solicitors, pilots, dentists, architects, scientists, engineers, geologists, MPs, vets, accountants, principals of private schools, and some of their staff. Some academics are Upper Middles, as are owners of successful businesses, especially those that sound at least vaguely professional. Public servants in the higher ranks.

Seriously Rich

Entrepreneurs — which can mean just about anything. Importers — can also mean anything, but tends to mean cheap tacky items from Asia. Successful businessmen — cars, manufactured goods. Restaurateurs, master builders, successful sportspeople, the more flamboyant medical specialists. Rock singers and TV soap opera stars. Anything to do with money (call yourself a stockbroker, investment adviser, whatever). Real estate, if selling expensive properties. (Otherwise real estate agents are Middle Australian or Lower Middle.)

Intellectuals

Professors, lecturers — anyone in a university from undergraduate to Vice-Chancellor. Writers, editors, publishers. Some teachers. Some professionals — especially anthropologists, archaeologists, psychologists. Anyone in the performing arts (except rock singers and TV actors).

Inner-City Sophisticates

Advertising, restaurants, the media — journalism, TV. Some actors and rock stars. Computers, sales, photography, fashion, design, decorating, some professionals.

Country

Grazier, farmer, stud breeder, vigneron, B&B proprietor. Stock and station agent, doctor, shopkeeper, hotelier, bank manager, vet.

Middle Australians

Middle managers, teachers, owners of small-to-medium retail businesses. Tradesmen who own their own business, especially the more technical ones — electricians, plumbers, carpenters. Public servants in the middle levels. Bank managers. Nurses, social workers, draftsmen, librarians and Ministers of Religion (except C of E — they're Upper Middle). As might be expected, people who are in the middle.

TWELVE

Nice car!

Real Aussies

Big old station wagon. If it's a V8 it's for you. If it's loud and fast and uses heaps of fuel, it's also for you. Lots of things dangling from mirrors or sitting in rear window — fluffy dice, nodding dogs with eyes that light up.

Lower Middles

The smaller, more economical cars. All the Datsun 120Ys in the land were bought by you and your friends. It is not uncommon for this class to keep its cars for twenty years. You look after them so well. Air freshener hanging from cigarette lighter.

Upper Middles

Volvo or Range Rover. It's a straight choice. Vehicles smell of dogs and rowing kit.

Seriously Rich

If younger — BMW. If older — Roller. Possibly Mercedes or Bentley, but these are considered very conservative and usually reserved for the aristocracy. Personalised number plates. Cars clean at all times.

Intellectuals

Virginia doesn't drive because cars are bad for the environment. That's why they live in a village-type suburb where she can walk everywhere. She also has a decrepit old bike with a wicker basket. Wolfgang walks around the neighbourhood but also drives an ancient Peugeot.

Inner-City Sophisticates

BMW Sports. Saab. Cabriolet. Whether you can afford it or not isn't the issue. Although you walk around the city and catch cabs (Dot would say taxi) more than any other class, the right car is still important. No children so cars always look perfect.

Country

Holden ute for local driving (that is, to the pub). Kelpie in the back as an optional extra. Large, comfortable station

John is amused by his inadvertent creation of a Toorak Tractor.

wagon for going to town. 4WDs are becoming more popular. For a long time you resisted because you didn't want to be mistaken for those poncy Toorak Tractor drivers. All vehicles filthy at all times.

Middle Australians

Large, fairly new-model Holden or Ford. Nothing sporty, flashy or falling apart. Value for money combined with comfort is your motto. If you have a lot of children then something like a Tarago. Cars usually clean, but messy with tennis racquets and school books.

THIRTEEN

So I said, mate, I said, mate.

One of the biggest of all class dividers is the way people speak. This can be a matter of accent, pronunciation or vocabulary. When people talk about an ocker they often mean someone with a broad Australian accent. When they say someone is a snob, they mean they talk with a so-called Upper Class accent, nowadays also known as an educated accent. There's no need to speak with a plum in your mouth, but do at least try to get it right.

TALK THE TALK

If you want to be taken for a higher class than you are, never say:

- *I done it. I seen it.*
- *Yous.* As in 'I'll see yous later.'
- *Them.* 'I'd like one of them ones.'
- *Me instead of 'my'.* 'Me kids, me car, me 'ouse.'
- *I could of (or would of, should of).* Say, 'I could have.'
- *Like.* 'There were, like, all of us, like, there, like.'
- *Comin' and goin'.* Another no-no.

- *Yeah.* Say yes.

- *Sekketry.* Should be secret'ri.

- *Esserdon.* Essendon is correct.

- Don't say *fore-head.* Say forrid.

- It's not *saint,* but s'nt.

- *Oz-tray-ya* is wrong. So is *Or-stray-lee-a.* It should be Oz-trayl-ya.

- *Somethink* and *anythink* are very wrong. Learn to say 'something' or 'anything'.

- *Aks* instead of 'ask' is (Country) Lower Class.

Sometimes keeping your mouth shut is the better option.

- *Pitcher*. Correct if you're talking about a water jug but not when you mean a painting or photograph.

- *Cassel* is Lower. Carstle is Upper. Likewise with dance, prance, glance . . .

- *Sandwich* is interesting. Lower Middles say sand-witch carefully, to avoid sounding like the really low classes who say sammidge. However, the Middles and Upper Middles say samwidge.

- *Either, neither.* These should rhyme with buy, not bee.

- *Envelope.* It is en, not on.

- *An hotel* is grammatically correct, but pedantic. To insist on it is Lower Middle.

- *Winder* is wrong if you mean window.

- *Fill-um*, when you mean film.

- *Know-en*, or *show-en* for known and shown.

- Don't end your sentences with *but*. 'It's good eh, but,' unless you're sending up either yourself or somebody else.

- Turning every sentence into a question — the infamous Aussie *rising inflexion* — is also a no-no.

Sometimes people will innocently comment on the pronunciation of a word. 'I thought it was . . .' There will always be someone else, usually Lower Middle, who will look knowing and say, 'It's all a matter of which school you went to.' Which school you went to is itself a euphemism for which class you belong to.

TRICK WORDS

Some words are more of a trap because they aren't incorrect grammatically, but nevertheless reveal your Lower Middle, poor or Real Aussie background.

Fiancé. Especially if you've lived together for five years and have three children. When you appear in the papers after the house has burnt down or your car has been stolen your mother will insist on you describing Gary as your fiancé to make it sound more respectable.

Fell pregnant. Fell by itself is even worse. 'I fell for Aaron when I was only nineteen.' (Apart from anything else, it's ambiguous.)

Frock. Too prissy. Say dress.

Passed away, passed on. (Lower Middle) — means 'died'.

Paid the supreme sacrifice — this means someone died in a war.

They repeat on me. This is another Lower Middle expression, used when someone eats something that causes them to fart or burp. It's not clear which meaning it is meant to convey, as most Lower Middles are too polite to explain.

Pardon. This seems to be a completely polite and innocuous word. The Upper Middles and Intellectuals will make fun of it all the same, preferring to bluntly say, 'What?'

WORDS YOU *SHOULD* SAY

One. 'One would almost think that ...'

Actually. 'Well actually I ...'

Ghastly. To describe practically anything disagreeable, from a mild inconvenience through to a major catastrophe.

AND FINALLY

Common. This useful little word is used by the different classes in different ways and is one you will have to understand. The so-called Upper Classes use it to mean 'not one of us', and apply it equally to men and women. However, the Lower Middles use it to mean risqué and it can be used in an extraordinary number of situations. Mostly though, they use it to describe women. 'She's a rather common little piece, I hear.' The dictionary defines it as: *ordinary, of little value, vulgar, of low degree.*

FOURTEEN

Ladies and gents

*The 'smallest room in the house' (typical Lower Middle
euphemism) is another indicator of class. What to call it?
'Toilet' is generally considered a Lower Class word.
'Lavatory' is upper class. Upper Middles, Intellectuals and
Middle Australians feel uncomfortable saying 'lavatory',
so have long said 'loo'. Estate agents say 'WC' or 'ensuite'.
Nikki says 'powder room'. Children of many classes and
the more truculent Real Aussies say 'dunny'. Teenagers say
'bog'. The ultimate in euphemisms, laughed at by
Australians of all classes, is the American 'bathroom'. Men
of all classes piss. Women wee. Children pee.*

Real Aussies

The Real Aussie toilet will be in the same browns and
oranges as the rest of the house — if Kev and Shar stay
there long enough the colours will come back into
fashion. An empty air-freshener container hangs on the
wall, next to Kev's rude calendar. It was he who gave Shar
the toilet-seat cover for Christmas — it's made of seas-
hells set into perspex. A little plastic stool for the kids
takes up most of the floor space and annoys Kev every
time he walks in. Farting jokes are amongst Kev's
favourites — he knows hundreds. Nothing to read.

Lower Middles

Dot's toilet is one of the main showpieces of her good housekeeping. It is tiled from top to bottom in very shiny new pale tiles and always spotlessly clean. The water is blue and the toilet roll has an attractive floral cover. There is also a matching toilet seat cover and mat shaped to fit the toilet bowl. A perpetual calendar noting all the family birthdays hangs on the wall. An air-freshener keeps any nasty smells at bay. The *Women's Weekly* to read.

Dot is kept busy in her never-ending battle
to keep nasty smells at bay.

Upper Middle

The loo says a lot about Caroline's taste. While not as ferociously clean as Dot's, it is a pretty room. Caroline isn't into the latest fashion colours but sticks with heritage green or burgundy. Dried flowers on the walls and framed originals of both Caroline and Richard's university degrees. *Time* magazine to read. A variety of cute soaps, and a hand-towel in the colour of the walls. Fittings in brass.

Seriously Rich

The main point is the high-tech engineering. Nikki's powder rooms (there are four) may be decorated in the stainless-steel, industrial style of the rest of the utility rooms in the house, but they are also designed for comfort. The seat will be warmed in winter and the loo itself doubles as a bidet. Nikki hadn't heard of them until she got married but now couldn't live without one. The toilet paper is printed with Nikki and Mike's initials.

Intellectuals

Wolfgang and Virginia's loo is at the back of their old house, off the verandah, and is as dusty and messy as the rest of the house. Virginia doesn't have time to bother with housework and in any case knows that material things don't matter. Recycled loo paper. Reading matter is the important thing — heavy going and confrontational.

Inner-City Sophisticates

The Inner-City Sophisticate's loo is as clean as Dot's, although the cleaning lady is responsible for it rather than Sascha. Nevertheless, both Si and Sascha spent days choosing the fittings and colours. Visitors now spend hours trying to find a button to press, as it is so cleverly blended into the décor. Witty framed cartoons and drawings by Si's advertising friends cover every wall.

Country

The country lavatory is a down-to-earth, old-fashioned no-nonsense place. It may even have an old-style chain-pull cistern. The basin will be a large china one, no plastic in sight. Sally provides unscented plain soaps such as Imperial Leather. A few prize ribbons for cattle and horses hang on the back of the door. Reading matter is a mixture of comic books, fertiliser manuals and the local rag.

Middle Australians

The Middle Australian WC is as middle of the road as everything else about them. Neither as clean as Dot's, as messy as Virginia's, as interesting as Caroline's, nor as advanced as Sascha's, it is fairly clean, has good quality soap and a basket for the spare toilet rolls. *National Geographics* to read and a scenic calendar on the wall.

FIFTEEN

'Does your Dad own a brewery?'

The divorce rate would be dramatically reduced if people only ever married within their own class. God knows, marriage is hard enough at the best of times. Men and women are not compatible by nature and have trouble sharing a house, bed and daily life. There is that constant tension between his desire to do exactly what he wants when he wants, and her futile wish to tame him. Marrying someone from another class takes this sex war to new heights. Most people who marry out of their class the first time learn from the experience and don't make the same mistake second time around.

On the other hand, one of the easiest ways to move up to a higher class is to marry someone from that class.

HOW TO TELL IF HE/SHE IS FROM ANOTHER CLASS

For women

You can be sure he is of a lower class than you if you suspect his mother matters more to him than you do. This is even more important than how he feels about his

Rebecca realises that Australia does indeed have a class system.

car. All men love their cars more than their wives or girlfriends, so it's not a true indicator.

He is of a class above yours if you buy a bottle of wine for his birthday dinner and he looks appalled and hides it before any guests appear.

For men

If you find yourself taking her to quiet little restaurants in obscure suburbs where no one is likely to know you (and you're not already married), she's of a lower caste.

If you want to change your entire lifestyle — get a different job, go to university or make a heap of money in a short time so you can impress her — you are the one feeling inferior.

If you miss these obvious signs your family's attitude will clear up any doubt. You will know from the minute you walk proudly in the door with your intended what the family think of him/her. Don't kid yourself that your family is free of class bias and that you can marry whom you like. Everyone wants their children to marry just slightly above them. Too low looks as though you were desperate and couldn't get anybody better. Too high is demoralising to your family. Your new spouse's family will barely tolerate yours at the wedding, and will ruthlessly exclude them afterwards.

THE IDEAL — MARRYING UP

For men

Men like to think they are the ones doing all the choosing and deciding and chasing. In fact, families will be closely examining them.

Do you know so and so?

The more Upper Class families ask this, in an attempt to find out who you are, although having to ask at all is an indication that as a prospect you have already failed the first test. Upper Middles and Uppers assume they already know anybody who would be suitable for their children.

What do you do?

Middle Classes. It means are you a layabout? Can you support our daughter? Will you be a liability — financial or otherwise?

Which is your university?

If the answer is none of them, you're in big trouble with the Intellectual family.

How many bags of wheat can you carry?

Country families will pose more physical tests. You will have to prove your worth through your actions — dig the car out of the bog, work in the sheepyards all day.
It all boils down to one thing. Is he one of us?

For girls

While girls still have to pass muster, there's no doubt it is easier for them to fake it. The right clothes can work wonders. Obviously these should always be discreet — no fishnet stockings when you're going to meet Mum, whatever class she is — but will be subtly different depending on circumstances.

If they seem Upper Middle you will have to bring out the Country Road, the small gold watch, the plain leather shoes and belt. Tie your hair back with a band, wear little make-up and don't talk too much. But don't appear shy either.

Wear Fletcher Jones if he's from the bush, and talk about your horses and dogs. You could wear the same outfit if he appears to be Middle Australian. If you suspect they have Intellectual leanings, then you can't go wrong with ethnic.

For an Inner-City Sophisticate man, you won't be dressing to please his family, who could be from any-where, but him. He will care about your clothes more than a man from any other class, probably more than a woman from any other class. He will expect you to be immaculately, smartly and expensively turned out at every moment of the day or night.

Similarly, if he's Seriously Rich his family could be from anywhere, so dress to please him. The difference between your man and the Inner-City Sophisticate is that yours will want you to look more sexy than smart. You will still have to pay a fortune for your clothes, but they need to be tighter, lower, brighter, golder.

SIXTEEN

'Do you fuck on first dates?'

AUSTRALIANS AND SEX

The Upper Middles and Middles make love, bonk or screw. Real Aussies (along with the really poor) talk about 'rooting' and 'fucking'. Intellectuals also use the word 'fuck' a lot. The clean-minded Middle Australians prefer to sleep with other people. Teenagers do 'it'.

Kev and Sharon were both fourteen when they did it for the first time, although not with each other. Sharon had an abortion at seventeen and married Kev at nineteen when she was pregnant with Jaylene. Kev isn't much of a lover but expects Sharon to feel like it whenever he does. Talking about it with his mates afterwards is almost the best part.

Dot and Brian waited until they were married; Dot likes to think of herself as a married virgin. Although Dot has never enjoyed it that much they have sex on a fairly regular basis because she thinks it's important to be available or Brian might be tempted to stray. Brian wishes Dot would sometimes take her nightie off beforehand.

Sharon wonders again whether marriage to Kev is worth the effort.

Caroline and Richard lived together before marrying. Caroline had a few relationships before she met Richard, although she didn't actually lose her virginity until she was twenty. Richard was considered quite a stud in his young days but is mostly faithful now, although if he does have an affair it will be with someone from their circle of friends, causing the maximum hurt and disruption. Their sex life is good, partly because Caroline constantly reads books to find ways of putting more zing into their love-making. Richard doesn't mind that, but he wishes she didn't want to be always talking about it.

Nikki keeps quiet about her past life — there were a few fairly wild years that she wouldn't want her children to know about. She's always afraid that some journalist is going to get hold of the photos and spill the beans. She and Mike have quite a good sex life — Nikki

knows she has to be inventive or Mike *will* stray —
again. Mike thinks he has a right to any girl who takes
his fancy.

Virginia and Wolfgang have never married, although even that hasn't been enough to keep Wolfgang
monogamous. They were there in the sixties, in spirit if
not in person, and believe that all sexual urges should be
acted on. Virginia lost her virginity at sixteen to a much
older man — it was part of her journey to find herself.
Both Virginia and Wolfgang understand that everybody is
naturally bisexual. They are prepared to go to jail to
defend the rights of their gay friends.

Si and Sascha talk about sex all the time, with their
friends and with each other. However, they are so busy
that it doesn't happen as often as they would like. It's also
a bit messy which is why they are more likely to use
condoms than anybody else. (Don't want to ruin the
perfect sheets.) Si is constantly being propositioned by
other men who think he must be gay. Both lost their
virginity, to other people, years ago when they were
living in the suburbs. It's not something they think about
much, seeing that that whole phase of their lives has
become a merciful blur.

John and Sally have a healthy attitude to sex. It's
not something dirty but a perfectly natural part of life. A
man works hard all day and needs sex at night. They
don't talk about it much but have sex often. John lost his
virginity on the seat of his Holden ute outside the local
hall one cold winter's night after a B&S ball. Sally's first
serious relationship happened when she was at teachers'
college. She thought she was in love and it took her years

to get over it. They rarely have affairs because everyone in the district would know.

Barb and Bob slept together before marriage but didn't live together. Barb hasn't slept with anybody else, although Bob had a few girlfriends. He took ages to screw up the courage to ask a girl to do it and secretly thinks he's always been a pretty ordinary lover. Barb sometimes wonders what it would be like with someone else.

SEVENTEEN

The billy-lids

Real Aussies

Have the most children of all, as well as the most highly vocal children. Whenever anyone suggests restricting the birth rate this class takes least notice. If not earning plenty of money there's always income support. Many complicated stepfamily situations — lots of half-brothers and sisters and several step-parents. Sharon yells her head off in the labour ward. Breastfeeds because bottles are too much trouble. Children named after TV characters or actors, or sports heroes. Also keen on anything a bit different — if there is an unusual or incorrect spelling of a name the ockers will use it: Kylie, Jason, Jai, Kailey.

Lower Middles

Generally only have two children, even if Catholic, so they can them give lots of time and attention, and because they only have enough bedrooms for two. Also because Brian is afraid of looking like a Real Aussie. Qualify for income support but wouldn't take it. Dot well-behaved in labour ward because zonked out on every drug available. A lot of talk afterwards about epidurals and episiotomies. Bottle feeds because it's easier to be organised. Children have nice old-fashioned names; often named after a favourite aunt or family friend. Janice, Clare, Ryan, Brendon.

Upper Middles

Two or at most three children. For some reason, very often a girl followed by a boy, although would prefer boy then girl so boy could escort sister to functions, and sister could meet brother's older friends. No more children because private schooling costs too much. Caroline has a natural birth — bonding is so important and it's all part of the noblesse oblige thing — anything too easy is suspect. Likewise with breastfeeding. It's a nuisance but has to be done. Children have old-fashioned English names. Nicholas, Sophie, Emily, James, Elizabeth, Charles.

Seriously Rich

May have lots of children (especially if Catholic). Can afford it, and need someone to carry on the business. The most expensive gynae in town, and every form of intervention that can be bought. Nikki breastfeeds for a month and then on to the bottle before nanny takes over. Children have dashing, sexy names: Roxane, Renee, Barbra, Scott, Rudi, Randy.

Intellectuals

Ideally — one child only. It's all so wearing, and Virginia never seems to become any more organised. Luckily,

Virginia realises the value of the one-child policy.

happen to believe in population containment, and also think that children develop more quickly if they have lots of adult time, not diluted by demands of other siblings. A home birth, or underwater. Will probably write a book about the experience afterwards. Breastfeeds until child starts school. Very unusual names: Xanthus, Ynez, Byron, Tristram, Abra, Athena.

Country

Three or four children, harking back to days when a large labour force was needed on the farm. Children quite self-reliant and sensible although may go through wild phase in teens and long for the city. At least one of the children born on the back seat of the car on the way to hospital, John having left it too late to leave. Easy births. Sally breastfeeds first child but falls away after that. Children have solid sensible names: Jack, Danny, Andrew, Julie, Jill.

Middle Australians

Three or four children. Family life is important. Can afford more than a couple of children because they have more money than the Lower Middles but don't consider private school to be essential. Barb has a caesarean. Tries breastfeeding but gives up after six weeks and turns to bottle with relief. Children often have biblical names, or are named after a character from a well-known book: Peter, Paul, Rachel, Linda, Wendy.

Inner-City Sophicsticates

Don't have children.

EIGHTEEN

The old school tie

Teachers are an interesting indicator of the class of an area. At some schools the track-suited parents rarely appear and when they do they are afraid of the teachers, whom they see as well-dressed professionals. At others, the professional parents look down, in the nicest way, on the teachers, who are well-meaning, of course, but, let's face it, losers.

GOVERNMENT OR NON-GOVERNMENT?

Do you send your child to a government school, or fork out the huge amounts of money needed for an independent school?

For some people, it isn't an issue. **Kev and Sharon** don't think of private schools, except to make rude remarks about them. Whether this is due to envy or ideological conviction only they know.

Dot and Brian can't afford the fees at an independent school, and in any case believe they would feel out of place. It never crosses their mind to even consider it.

On the other hand, **Caroline and Richard** wouldn't dream of sending their children to a government school. They send them to the same private school they went to. The grandparents may pay all or some of the fees, or Richard will have set up some sort of financial scheme when the children were born.

Those aspiring to be Upper Middle are prepared to forego food or essential medical treatment to be able to afford private school fees. They choose a middle-of-the-range private school near their home. It's one of the chief steps up the ladder, but they don't want to go straight for the top schools because they haven't yet learnt all the rules of the game and they don't want to appear incongruous or conspicuous.

Nikki and Mike go for the most expensive school in their state. What's the point of having all that money if you can't buy the best? They haven't had the children's names down since birth, if they've just made the money, but a large donation to the building fund does wonders.

Barb and Bob face a dilemma. With a certain amount of sacrifice on their part they could pay the fees, but they wonder if it's worth it. Until recently the academic record of our most famous schools was nothing to write home about, and Barb suspects that drugs are at least as bad in the private schools as in the government, and may even be worse, given that the students have more money and arrogance.

However, as the fee-paying schools rise to the top of the exam results league tables, more Middle Australian parents choose to go that route. This often means that

Barb has to go back to work to find the money. Some times this results in the Middle Australian family deciding to go the whole hog and become Upper Middle.

John and Sally face similar choices. If they're Upper Middle they will naturally send the children to their old school like their city cousins, although it will cost them even more, because they have to pay for boarding fees as well. If they're Real Aussie or Lower Middle, their children will go to the local secondary school with no further ado. Country-based Middle Australians agonise between the local school — hopeless, private boarding school — expensive, or a compromise like a city high school that has a hostel attached. Sometimes mothers go to live in the city for several years to supervise the children's schooling.

Wolfgang and Virginia face the biggest dilemma of all. They naturally don't believe in the élitist ethos of the private school, nor the fact that most of them profess to be religious schools, but neither do they want their children to miss out on a good education. Certainly they want the children to know and admire the poor and to fight for their rights, but not to the extent that their education is held back because the government school teacher is too busy trying to keep the students from killing each other to actually find time to teach anything.

They also want their children to have access to all that marvellous music in the private schools. What many of them end up doing is sending the children to the local primary school — which, after all, isn't going to be in a hideous bland outer suburb because they wouldn't live there in the first place — and then make sure the children win a scholarship to a good private secondary school. They either put their principles on hold for the time the children are at school, or give up and become Upper Middle themselves.

A group of like-minded Intellectuals may also get together and start their own school, which will be founded on the highest ideals of co-operative learning, but end up floundering because nobody does any actual work. Wolfgang and Virginia quickly realise that if the children are going to have any hope of getting into university they will have to try something else, so arrange for them to win a scholarship to the best selective government school in their state.

Si and Sascha don't have this problem because they don't have children.

CATHOLIC SCHOOLS

There is one other option, and that is the Catholic system.

The top fee-paying Catholic schools are little different from the other independent schools, and are available only to the rich, but it's a different story with the Catholic systemic schools. If you really are a Catholic there's no problem — you send your children to the local parish school, pay the low fees, and get all the benefits of uniforms and the promise of discipline. Although Catholics traditionally haven't been at the top of the social tree in Australia, some aspiring Upper Middles envy them their natural entrée to a fee-paying system.

If you're not Catholic you can put yourself in something of an awkward situation by opting for this system. For a start, your child might feel like a pariah because they don't know the things the other kids know. Secondly, you may end up giving your child an inferior education because these schools are bursting at the seams.

Even more importantly, you can look ridiculous to everyone else because it's so obvious you are trying to aspire to what you can't afford. Is it worth it, given that the social life associated with these schools is not that exciting? You are also going to be irritated every time you go to the school and see all the mothers in their tight black pants, frilly blouses and teased peroxide hair.

It's up to you but if you want a private education for your children — and if you want to be Upper Middle it's essential — there's really nothing for it but to take out a loan, get a second job, or make sure your children win scholarships.

PUBLIC VERSUS PRIVATE: USEFUL INFORMATION

The term 'public school' causes confusion. Nikki knows that while it would appear to mean government school, as in public funding, paid for by taxes, free to everyone, 'public school' in England can mean private school. Because she doesn't want to appear ignorant, she tries to avoid using the word 'private' school. But neither does

Caroline understands the importance of being involved in her children's education.

she want any misunderstanding regarding the fact that Rudi is in fact at a very expensive school. If she says in conversation that, 'My son is at a public school' there is always the risk that Mrs Seriously Rich will believe that Rudi is going to the government school up the street.

The truth is that only a very few of the English non-government schools are correctly known as public schools, for complicated historical reasons (see below).

Likewise, not one school in Australia qualifies to call itself a public school, in the English sense, so when anyone describes a school like Geelong Grammar as a 'public' school they are incorrect.

More and more people use the words independent school to indicate a non-government, fee-paying school, and government school to describe the so-called free schools that are run and funded by the state.

English public schools

Apparently paradoxically, they are the very oldest and richest of the schools — Eton, Harrow, Rugby, Winchester, Shrewsbury, Charterhouse, St Paul's, Westminster and Merchant Taylor's. The many newer, independent, fee-paying schools which appeared over time were *not* public schools but, strictly speaking, private schools. They were also sometimes referred to, incorrectly, as minor public schools.

NINETEEN

Aussies do IT

KEV AND SHARON

Like the Seriously Rich, you believe in the motto that big is beautiful. You have at least one large TV that shows brightly coloured people and has a particularly high volume setting. As well, there are other TVs and VCRs scattered around the house at various spots. They will be second-hand, or lent by a mate who is overseas, or bought by the children themselves, provoking World War Three if anyone else dares to watch their TV. Mostly, they will be tuned to sports stations, or used to show rented videos. These will be very loud, with much sex and violence.

Real Aussie women are ridiculed for watching daytime TV, but it's the only time Mavis can get her hands on the remote control, or hear the TV at all above the din everyone is making. When she gets the chance, Sharon likes to watch sad romantic movies.

Kev and Shar don't often listen to the radio, but Donny does, all the time. He carries a large black radio on his shoulder, sharing his taste in music with all and sundry. Likewise his car radio is set permanently at full volume and played with the windows down, the noise drowning out the throb of the V8.

There is an old stereo system sitting in a corner of the lounge room, but it's impossible to hear anything played on it above the racket coming from the loud rock music being played by Jaylene and Aaron and their mates.

Computers are for playing games.

DOT AND BRIAN

The record-player is starting to look a little worn nowadays, and people look at you in an amused way when you try to buy parts for it. But you love music. Dot can put on a record — perhaps *The Sound of Music* — when she is ironing or sewing.

The radio is also very important. There is one in the kitchen, so Dot can listen to all her favourite talkback shows and ring up to win the competitions. Brian has another in the workshop and can follow the cricket score when he's woodworking.

You don't need a computer. What would you do with it? Even Lower Middle children don't need one; their sport and ballet take up too much of their time, and as it is it will take you all your efforts to pay off the set of encyclopedias to help them with their homework.

TV is another matter. Brian likes to think that he is finally having an influence on *something* when, as a *TV Week* reader, he gets to vote for the TV awards. Dot finds the summer very long without her favourite soap operas.

Dot and Brian also watch the news religiously, to see what is happening with crime in their state. Usually, it's appalling (especially as the only news the commercial stations show is local crime), but with any luck there will be a rally advertised where they can make a statement along with other like-minded decent citizens.

CAROLINE AND RICHARD

Despite your penchant for things old, you are very keen on IT. Everybody in the family has their own computer. The kids use theirs for homework and games. Caroline uses hers for study and to trace the family history. Richard for work and games.

Upper Middles also have a very good sound system. Classical music is an important part of the image. Also jazz. It's one of the things you have in common with the Intellectuals.

You watch TV, especially the news and documentaries. The only station Caroline and Richard admit to watching regularly is the ABC, particularly for the news. In actual fact they often sneak over to the other channels for sport and movies, and it's Sophie and Nicholas who watch the ABC most — all that marvellous satiric comedy. You have several TVs and VCRs — at least one for the adults and one for the children. They will be of a good quality and size without being vulgar.

When Richard is away on business Caroline and the children go to the video shop and hire all their favourite movies.

NIKKI AND MIKE

You have the very latest sound system, but then you have such a large collection of music. All your rock-star friends give you copies of their latest albums and video clips. Every room in the house has a giant TV screen, even though you also have the mini movie theatre. One of your favourite entertainments is to invite people over to see the latest (as in pre-release) movies.

Computers are essential for the business. Nikki never touches it but Mike is well up with the latest technology.

The only time Nikki listens to the radio is through headphones when she is walking or working out.

Nikki manages the family's hectic social calendar.

VIRGINIA AND WOLFGANG

In general you avoid anything that uses too much power or isn't natural. However, you must have your good computers — it makes it easier to prepare the protest letters. In any case, they are essential for Virginia's writing.

Another essential is the sound system. Your taste is similar to the Upper Middles' — classical and jazz — but more aggressively so. They tend to be geared towards the school recital, while you attend every musical event possible. Classical and jazz of course — Richard would no more think of attending a popular stage show than of flying to the moon.

Intellectuals also have a TV and VCR. Only one of each, because you don't really approve. In many ways you wish you were brave enough to take a stand against the blatant commercialism and mindlessness of most of what's offered, but you're not. However, you do monitor closely what the children watch. That's another reason for having only the one child.

In any case, you don't believe in the children being off in a separate room. They must be with adults as much as possible to develop them socially. You also expect them to be interested in the same programmes as you. The ABC and SBS only, although the ABC has tested your allegiance in recent years.

Certainly the SBS news is the only one worth watching, even though you do watch the ABC too. However, it makes you so furious to see what the government is doing to stuff up the country, and ignoring the people who matter (that is, the poor and indigenous).

Radio: as for TV. Quality programmes — music, current affairs — on the non-commercials.

SASCHA AND SI

You also have a very modern sound system, and a large collection of music. As well as classical, it features the more sophisticated and unusual popular singers. Piano music is also a good choice. It tinkles away elegantly in the background as you entertain, but doesn't strain anybody's thinking powers too much.

Both Sascha and Si use computers for work, and understand and admire technology. They have plenty of room for a home office, with the three bedrooms and no children, but the office doesn't get used all that much — Sascha and Si are always out. Likewise the TV is there, but they don't often watch it. They prefer to find out what's happening from talking to people.

SALLY AND JOHN

Ignorant city people would be amazed to see how you have embraced information technology, forgetting that you've always known about machinery and this is a logical extension. The computer is invaluable for the farm accounts, planning, and communication. Sally and John feel they need it more than anybody. Their kids can't easily whiz around to the local library.

You like TV, especially for sport, but the weather dictates what you will watch. On clear nights you can get anything, but often you watch your favourite programmes through a blur of white snow. You have a great fondness for the ABC, who were the first to bring TV to the bush. *Bellbird* set a standard for Australian drama that has never been matched, in your opinion. Even today, whatever you are watching, you are quite likely to spend half your time recognising old characters from *Bellbird*. You can remember exactly what was happening in your life at the time when Charlie fell off the wheat silo. *Blue Hills* led to *Bellbird* led to *A Country Practice* led to *Blue Heelers*.

However, it is the radio that is most important. Work and meal times have to fit around *The Country Hour*, which broadcasts in the middle of the day. Sally becomes incensed at having to sit silently throughout lunch because John is intent on hearing prices and weather reports.

BARB AND BOB

As in most things, you tend to be in the middle. Like the Upper Middles, you have at least two TVs, one for the adults and one for the children. You watch all channels except SBS. Barb likes the Sunday night movie and the medical dramas. Bob watches sport and a few documentaries. They both watch the news every night, as a ritual, although don't get as incensed by it as either the Intellectuals or the Lower Middles. After all, most of it is going to make very little difference to their life.

Barb and Bob have two computers, one for the children because they want them to do well at school and they know that computer skills are an essential these days, and one for the business. Bob likes to feel he knows a bit about computers — it's a blokey thing — but Barb has enough trouble setting the VCR; she has no desire to learn about computers.

Depending on the era when you bought the stereo system it will be either silver or black glass, sitting on a small table. You have a broad range of music from light classics to marching tunes to ballads to Neil Diamond. You are, after all, the Middle Class, the class of reason, the bridge between all the other classes.

There is a radio in the kitchen which Barb listens to fairly regularly.

TWENTY

The great Australian novel

KEV AND SHARON

Your house has almost no books, nor do you have newspapers delivered. Kev reads magazines that have either pictures of cars or girls in them. Sharon reads women's magazines and the same romance novels that Dot loves.

DOT AND BRIAN

You usually read your local daily newspaper, and always read your free neighbourhood weekly, turning first to the section that brings you up to date on crime in your suburb. It's also useful to be able to hear about any new neighbourhood watch or protest groups that are being organised.

Dot reads romances by the dozen, swapping and sharing them about with her friends. She also reads a whole range of women's magazines, although her favourites have changed their character so much lately she hardly knows where she is. They still carry their stories about the royals which is a comfort, but in general they have become more and more vulgar. Instead of nice stories about ordinary people, and interesting biographies of film stars, they go in for sex so much more.

Brian doesn't read a lot, except for the *Reader's Digest*, but he does have a few books about carpentry and gardening.

CAROLINE AND RICHARD

Caroline likes reading just as much as Virginia does, but has less time to indulge herself.

When they get the chance, Upper Middles read as many newspapers as possible. Caroline especially reads the literary sections, and Richard the business and financial bits. Both also read magazines — Richard the more factual and international ones, Caroline the literary and lifestyle.

Both have books piled up next to their bed. Caroline usually has three or four books going at once — the one she has to read for her book club meeting next week, a biography, a lighter novel which she feels guilty about, and some sort of serious book — meditation or women's issues. She also loves anything by Nancy Mitford or Jilly Cooper.

Richard reads less than Caroline, finding time for only a few long books a year, which he describes in detail to everyone he meets.

Science fiction is OK, and for some reason so are murder mysteries, provided you make a point of saying that you find them a great means of escape from your demanding and stressful job.

Children's books are important. You must have copies of *The Wind in the Willows*, *The Secret Garden*, *Little Women* and, to be patriotic, *Seven Little Australians*.

NIKKI AND MIKE

You don't so much read newspapers and magazines as appear in them. Nor do you read books very often. Only bores have time to read.

However, Nikki buys the glossies to keep up to date with her mates, and for a long flight will pick up the occasional airport book with gold lettering. Mike is kept busy reading the financial news.

VIRGINIA AND WOLFGANG

Both read day and night. It's not only an essential for your work, it's as vital to your well-being as eating and drinking. However, if deprived of reading matter for all but the shortest time, you will make up for it by writing something yourselves.

You read the literary magazines, national news-papers and journals and any quality international news-papers you can get hold of.

The right book is important for the aspiring Intellectual. No more lolling around with a light maga-zine or romance. Novels should be post-modern and extremely difficult to read. If the book keeps jumping

Virginia comes 'this close' to finding the perfect phrase.

from place to place and the sentences are almost impossible to decipher, you know you're on the right track. Likewise for poetry. On the whole, however, you're safer to stick with heavy non-fiction, especially politics (left-wing only), science or philosophy. History is all right as long as it's not from the point of view of the white colonials. Neither Virginia nor Wolfgang would ever dream of joining a book club because they know the discussion would be at such a low level it would drive them insane.

Intellectuals will go without food to be able to afford the right book.

SI AND SASCHA

You do much of your reading in cafés — the newspapers with breakfast, and magazines at any other time. You also buy quite a few of the smarter fashion and food magazines so you are right up with the current look.

You also read a surprising number of books — always the latest pseudo-literary book that everyone is talking about, or else a new author whom you happen to know personally. Not having children and travelling quite a lot, you actually have more time to read than most of the other classes, despite your hectic social life.

Both Si and Sascha loved *Bonfire of the Vanities*, especially the first part. It summed up everything they want to be.

SALLY AND JOHN

John reads farming magazines and machine manuals. Very occasionally, perhaps when dragged away for a holiday and feeling bored, he might read a Western.

Sally reads a lot. With the lousy TV reception and no near neighbours it's a great source of contact with others' ideas, and she loves her book club meetings. She also enjoys the women's magazines.

BARB AND BOB

The daily newspaper is delivered. Bob reads it before work and Barb reads it during the day once everyone has gone. She also buys a lot of magazines, some the same as Dot and some that Caroline likes.

She reads a lot of books — neither too heavy nor too light. They must have a plot, believable characters, and an interesting theme, but still be readable. In the past few years she joined a book club and has read more and more literary fiction. It's almost as good as doing a university degree, and the supper afterwards is half the fun. She wouldn't miss it for anything.

Bob reads less, particularly as he gets older, but likes a book that tells a good yarn now and then. Someone like Wilbur Smith. He also reads car and fishing magazines.

TWENTY-ONE

... and an emu up a gum tree — Christmas

DOT AND BRIAN

One of the high points of the year (apart from The Wedding). The tree comes out of its box six weeks before Christmas and everyone helps to decorate it. It sits in the front window with its lights flashing. The wreath goes up on the front door at the same time, and the tinsel is draped across the lounge room. It's a busy time — Dot spends weeks baking the pudding and cakes, and hanging the cards on a string across the window. Getting the house set up to win the Christmas lights street competition is the major undertaking for Brian. You're talking serious money and work.

KEV AND SHARON

A tinsel tree like the Lower Middles, but that's it. You couldn't be bothered fiddling around putting up all those lights and decorations. Nor can Sharon see the point in cooking everything herself when there is perfectly good food in the shops. Real Aussies do, however, buy more presents than all the other classes put together. These are

Bringing Christmas cheer to the whole neighbourhood.

piled up under the tree and at the crack of dawn the children tear in, rip off all the paper in one go, try all the presents, break one immediately and then whine for the next three days. A noisy day. A lot of children, a lot of loud adult voices, a lot of beer drunk, and a family fight at some stage.

CAROLINE AND RICHARD

The Tree is the key to it all. It must be green, large, and real. Those dreadful silver tinsel things that were around for ages were the height of vulgarity, while the green (but artificial) ones which have replaced them are, if anything, worse. For you, it must be a real tree. Living is best

— after all, you are into saving the environment — but a dead one is OK as long as it's whole. It's not so much that you like real trees; frankly they're a bore, dropping needles all over the floor, and needing watering every five minutes, but you have no choice. Silver tinsel would drop you down a class or two within minutes. It's one of the class indicators. Food is a mix of traditional and high-quality contemporary. Lots of seafood. Good wines. Christmas is a lot of work because everyone comes to your house every year.

NIKKI AND MIKE

Christmas means Parties. You give or go to one practically every night for two months or so either side of the day. Masses of champagne drunk, and enormous amounts of food eaten. You will also spend a fortune on presents, receive and send a couple of hundred cards — you have so many friends — and get into the papers on a couple of occasions. The day itself is a bit of an anticlimax. Nikki's family, frankly, are something of an embarrassment, but it's the one day you can't leave them out altogether. The tree is a specially grown 40ft high living pine tree.

SASCHA AND SI

Generally speaking you will be going home to the family in another state for Christmas. It's convenient to have somewhere to go so that at all the parties in the week before Christmas you can say, 'I'm really longing to see the family. It will be so exciting. We're all getting together. Yes, I'm flying out on Friday night.' You know the whole thing will be a crashing bore from start to finish, but because it's all happening far away nobody else has to know. Sascha does put up a tree — a real tree painted silver, with fruit and vegetables piled up under it as decoration.

JOHN AND SALLY

Mostly a battle between men and women as to whether the men will be able to participate at all. If harvest isn't finished Christmas will have to be cancelled. A quick dash to the city for shopping, and to bring the children home from boarding school if Upper Middle. The concert and tree at the local school is the big social occasion. Everyone goes, but the men fall asleep during prize giving. Plenty of food and cold beer on the day. Everyone falls asleep in the afternoon under a tree, on the verandah, wherever. A swim in the pool, lake, river, dam at some stage. Boxing Day is sports day — often tennis or cricket.

BARB AND BOB

For you it's a dead pine branch or a Norfolk Island pine. The Norfolk Islands are a bit spindly, but once you've covered them with decorations they look OK. It is also increasingly OK to go for an artificial tree, but it must be large, green and expensive. At night you can't tell the difference. The cards are standing on the sideboard where they blow off in the wind every time someone opens a door. Lots of food — the traditional turkey, ham and pudding. The family around the tree to open presents. The one time in the year that Bob goes to church.

WOLFGANG AND VIRGINIA

Don't believe in Christmas.

TWENTY-TWO

Getaway

Kev and Sharon travel fairly often. Not being too worried about long-term security, they head off on a brief cheap package tour any time they can scrape together enough cash to pay for the ticket. Dot and Brian rarely leave the country, but may save up for the one big (tourist class) trip of a lifetime to see their relatives in the UK. The Upper Class and the Seriously Rich travel virtually all the time, Uppers because it's just what they do, the Seriously Rich because they can. They think the expression 'First Class' sums them up very nicely.

Caroline and Richard travel for business and culture (business class), Virginia and Wolfgang also for culture of one sort or another, often connected with post-graduate study. Barb and Bob travelled when they were young, and once they've retired go on the occasional tour to Europe or America. Sally and John do the same. Si and Sascha travel a lot — no kids, pets or garden to tie them down.

FAVOURITE DESTINATIONS

Kev and Sharon

A camping trip — at the beach or by the river. You set up a big messy camp and drink a lot of beer. Also fish and play cards. Everybody drops in. Increasingly, however, to Bali, Fiji or the Gold Coast.

Dot and Brian

You take the caravan to the same place you've been going to every year for the last twenty years. Either by the beach, or more likely, a fishing spot on a river. When Brian retires you buy a bigger caravan and head off around Australia. The main point is not seeing the country but experiencing the culture of the caravan parks — every night is party night with like-minded people. Those who go north every year to escape the winter make a point of leaving on the Thursday before Easter when the roads are full of frustrated workers trying to get away for a few days — it adds to the feeling of holiday excitement.

Caroline and Richard

Go in for lots of smaller breaks. One or two overseas business trips every year. One overseas holiday — perhaps Japan, skiing in Canada, trekking in Nepal. One summer break at your own or a friend's beach house. One other country holiday in spring or autumn — a friend's country house or a chalet by a lake. Skiing in winter if a skiing family. For what's left of the year you make do with short breaks at upmarket bed and breakfasts in pretty spots around the country.

Nikki and Mike

The main object is the travelling from house to house. There's not much point buying a London townhouse, a New York apartment or a Tuscan villa if you never go there. Also go to wherever is the latest 'in' place around the world — pity it's getting harder and harder to find somewhere that isn't being torn apart by wars. Skiing, obviously, both in Australia and other countries. Glamorous hotels in other cities for short breaks. Summer holidays means Noosa or Palm Beach. Quieter places like Mt Eliza are more Upper Class and harder to break into.

Wolfgang and Virginia

Don't go on conventional family holidays as such. No fishing from a lake or building sand castles on a beach. However, sipping wine from a friend's balcony is OK. Also, extended travelling through exotic countries by local transport is much admired. Exotic means one that hasn't yet been discovered by the masses. Sleeping on the beach in Bali was bliss in the early seventies, but a modern-day package tour is not you. Likewise you hitched around Europe when you were young but have no intention of ever going on a bus tour of Europe, America or anywhere else for that matter. India is always fascinating.

Si and Sascha

You like to rent a beach house somewhere glamorous. It must be within reach of at least one good restaurant and, it goes without saying, have access to such amenities as electricity and sound plumbing. The acid test is that if Sascha can't use her hair dryer it's too far from civilisation. Also snow skiing — it's physical but glamorous; nature with style. Travel means cities — New York — as often as you can. The energy is so infectious. LA, London, Paris, Rome, Hong Kong.

John and Sally

Two weeks at the beach in the summer. The women and kids take a house and the men come and go when they can — it's fire season. Also like to take four-wheel-drive trips through the centre or up to the Gulf. You go to Europe at least once, but aren't very interested in anywhere else. Summer beach holiday

Barb and Bob

Like Dot and Brian, you go to the same spot every year but it's more likely to be a rented house than a caravan or tent. Also more likely to be by the sea than a river. Somewhere where the kids can swim and surf and mess around in boats and join in the local scene — prawning or crabbing or whatever it may be. Another favourite holiday is going to stay with relatives on their farm. One good holiday a year.

THE BEACH HOLIDAY

Surprisingly, some places are popular with all the classes. The difference is that the Upper Classes are in the expensive apartments overlooking the water and the others are in the camping ground set well back from any views. More likely, a resort will be exclusive to one class or other. Palm Beach is only for the rich. If you want to get on in the social scene, you don't go to Rosebud.

Another difference is that to the Lower Classes this is the big week of the year. To the Upper Classes this is not a vacation; this is just a rest. Make it clear that you are here strictly to recover from your busy year and to catch up with all your friends in a relaxed way.

The Upper Classes leave town on Boxing Day and congregate in their favourite places — whole suburbs virtually transplanted to an expensive beachside location. They appear in the gossip columns just the same, looking as groomed and coiffed as ever, even though wearing bathers and a suntan rather than ball dresses and suits.

Sascha takes in the sights.

Beach behaviour

Kev and Sharon sit where they like on the beach and play their music loudly. Bloody hell, they've got just as much right as anybody else to be there, haven't they? Nobody owns the bloody sand. Do yer wanna make a thing of it, mate? They buy pies and chips and cans of Coke. The kids swim outside the flags and endanger everyone around them by doing bombies off the jetty.

It's a major expedition for Dot and Brian to spend a day at the beach. They have a large umbrella, an Esky, towels, floats for the kids, hats, suncream and a complete change of clothes for everybody. They take all their own food (sandwiches) and drink (cold cordial) because it's so expensive to buy. Brian spends the next week getting sand out of the car.

Richard and Caroline mostly go to the beach when they're staying at the holiday shack. Richard goes down early in the morning for a refreshing swim and Caroline goes later with a towel, the raffia hat and a book. Sophie, Nicholas and Emma all love the beach and spend several years of their lives practically living there.

Mike is only interested in seeing the ocean from his yacht, but Nikki quite enjoys a morning alone on the beach. It's less boring to work on the tan where there's something to watch, rather than by the pool at home. She can perv on the hunks in their Speedos and chat with her friends on the phone at the same time.

If Sascha has a rare free day she likes to go to the beach to show off her figure in her new bathers. Her towel, bag, hat and glasses are incredibly smart and she looks like a magazine advertisement as she carefully applies an expensive sun lotion. Si isn't keen on the beach. There's something so primeval about it that he doesn't feel comfortable.

John can't get excited about the beach or beach holidays at all. Having grown up inland, he learned to swim in dams, rivers and lakes, and can't understand Sally's enthusiasm for sand and surf. She insists, however, because she wants the children to grow up with happy beach holiday memories similar to her own.

Bob hates the beach except for fishing, so Barb goes with a friend. It makes her feel quite young and carefree to bodysurf amongst all the young people, and she feels it must be good for the figure. She gets a good tan but bores the kids by telling them every year about how when she was twelve she used to coat herself with vinegar and olive oil, and then peel off the skin after she burnt.

Wolfgang and Virginia never lie on beaches. Wolfgang is sure that nobody ever had an original thought while lying mindlessly on hot sand, and Virginia knows what her body would look like out of the caftan.

TWENTY-THREE

Four-legged friends

Real Aussies

Dogs mostly. Rottweiler, pit bull terrier. Loud, aggressive and dangerous. Similar to your car.

Lower Middles

Scotch terrier. Anything small and yapping. Guinea pigs. Cats will be very highly bred and probably hairless (less mess).

Upper Middles

Dogs — labrador, golden retriever or King Charles spaniel. Something you can take on a lead to the regatta.

Seriously Rich

Clipped poodle.

Intellectuals

Probably nothing, but if anything, perhaps surprisingly, cats. Virginia could well end up as an eccentric old woman with wild hair and twenty starving moggies.

Sally knows the meaning of true companionship.

Country

Sheepdogs and horses. The loss of a horse is almost as tragic as losing a child.

Middle Australians

Dogs and cats. Cats will be moggies or fluffy long-hairs. Dogs — perhaps labrador, often German Shepherd. Also rabbits.

Inner-City Sophisticates

None, obviously.

TWENTY-FOUR

Up there, Cazaly!

Real Aussies

Spectator sports — football and car racing. Fishing and pool. The kids play basketball.

To Mavis and her friends, loyalty and hero-woship are more than simply words.

Lower Middles

Netball, hockey, bowls, soccer.

Upper Middles

Rugby, rowing, tennis, squash, cricket, snow and water skiing.

Seriously Rich

Snow skiing, yachting, working out, flying light planes, driving fast cars.

Inner-City Sophisticates

Squash, working out, swimming laps, skiing.

Country

Polocrosse, tennis, cricket. Follow the local footy team.

Middle Australians

Tennis, swimming, golf, water skiing, fishing.

Intellectuals

Not interested.